AI MADE FOR YOU

YOUR ESSENTIAL GUIDE TO GENERATIVE AI, LLMS, PROMPT ENGINEERING, AND THE RISE OF AGI

KIRAN MAADAMSHETTI, FMVA®, CSPO®, CBE®

Copyright © KIRAN MAADAMSHETTI, FMVA®, CSPO®, CBE®
All Rights Reserved.

This book has been self-published with all reasonable efforts taken to make the material error-free by the author. No part of this book shall be used, reproduced in any manner whatsoever without written permission from the author, except in the case of brief quotations embodied in critical articles and reviews.

The Author of this book is solely responsible and liable for its content including but not limited to the views, representations, descriptions, statements, information, opinions and references ["Content"]. The Content of this book shall not constitute or be construed or deemed to reflect the opinion or expression of the Publisher or Editor. Neither the Publisher nor Editor endorse or approve the Content of this book or guarantee the reliability, accuracy or completeness of the Content published herein and do not make any representations or warranties of any kind, express or implied, including but not limited to the implied warranties of merchantability, fitness for a particular purpose. The Publisher and Editor shall not be liable whatsoever for any errors, omissions, whether such errors or omissions result from negligence, accident, or any other cause or claims for loss or damages of any kind, including without limitation, indirect or consequential loss or damage arising out of use, inability to use, or about the reliability, accuracy or sufficiency of the information contained in this book.

Made with ♥ on the Notion Press Platform
www.notionpress.com

To my mother, whose love and wisdom have shaped me into who I am
today.

To my father, whose strength and guidance have been a constant source of
inspiration.

To my wife, for her unwavering support, patience, and encouragement in
every step of this journey.

To my brother, for always being there, sharing laughter, and providing the
camaraderie that only siblings can.

And to my son, the light of my life, whose innocence and joy remind me
every day of the beauty and wonder of the world.

With deepest gratitude and love.

Contents

Contents

WELCOME

It was a quiet November day in 2022, and the world was about to change in a way few could have imagined. On that day, **OpenAI introduced ChatGPT** to the world—a new kind of artificial intelligence that could do more than just follow instructions. It could *converse, create,* and *think* in ways that felt startlingly human. What happened next was nothing short of a revolution.

I remember the first time I heard about it. It wasn't just another AI tool. It was something different. People were talking about how it could write essays, answer questions, generate code, and even compose poetry. "Could this really be true?" I wondered. Could an AI understand language well enough to carry on a conversation that felt natural?

Soon, the floodgates opened. People across the globe were eager to try ChatGPT. They began asking it questions—anything from "What's the weather like today?" to "Can you write a poem about the moon?" And with each interaction, the world started to realize that something extraordinary was happening.

The Awakening: "Is This Really Possible?"

At first, many of us were skeptical, testing ChatGPT with playful curiosity. "Let's see how good this thing really is," we thought. People started asking it trivial questions, seeking quick answers, and were left stunned by its ability to respond in a way that sounded intelligent, coherent, and often *human.* I remember my first experience: I asked it to explain quantum physics in simple terms. Not only did it break it down easily, but it made me *want* to learn more.

From there, the magic happened. It wasn't just about answers. It was about possibilities. ChatGPT could generate ideas in a flash, craft entire essays, and even troubleshoot problems. As businesses, students, and creators dived in, they found a tool that could help them work smarter and faster than ever before.

The Transformation: ChatGPT in Everyday Life

In Education: For students, ChatGPT wasn't just a tool—it became a study companion. Imagine having a tutor available 24/7, able to explain a complex concept in seconds. Homework became easier to manage, and research projects were completed with a few prompts. But it wasn't just for students; teachers used it to explain concepts in a more engaging way, and parents found it to be a great educational resource for kids.

In the Workplace: Think about your daily grind. Emails, reports, presentations—tasks that used to take hours could now be completed in minutes. Professionals turned to ChatGPT to draft content, generate reports, or even brainstorm ideas. But beyond the efficiency, something deeper was happening: ChatGPT wasn't just helping us *work* faster, it was changing *how* we worked. It acted as a creative partner, a personal assistant, and a problem-solver—all rolled into one.

In Creative Industries: Writers, musicians, and artists alike were astounded by how ChatGPT could spark new ideas. A novelist could now ask it to brainstorm plot twists, a songwriter could explore lyric ideas, and a graphic designer could find inspiration for their next big project. But the real breakthrough wasn't about replacing creativity—it was about *augmenting* it. ChatGPT became a co-creator, pushing the boundaries of what was possible in art and content.

The Ripple Effect: Shaking the Status Quo

As more people began to use ChatGPT, its impact became undeniable.

In Customer Service: Businesses realized they could revolutionize customer support with AI. ChatGPT could handle inquiries, answer questions, and resolve issues faster than ever before. For customers, this meant quicker responses and better experiences. For companies, it meant efficiency and cost savings.

In Healthcare: Imagine having an AI assistant that could help you manage your health. ChatGPT wasn't diagnosing diseases, but it could help you understand symptoms, suggest healthy habits, and guide you through medical information. This created an accessible bridge to health education, making it easier for everyone to be informed and proactive about their well-being.

In Finance: People began using ChatGPT to help manage their money. Whether it was tracking spending, analyzing investment options, or creating budgets, this AI-powered tool made personal finance more accessible. It was no longer just for finance professionals—it was for everyone.

The Turning Point: What's Next?

However, not everyone shared the excitement. As ChatGPT grew more powerful, so did the fears. Could it replace jobs? Would it cause a loss of human creativity? What about privacy and ethics? These concerns were valid. As AI became more integrated into our lives, society was forced to confront its challenges.

But here's the twist: ChatGPT wasn't about replacing humans—it was about enabling us. It wasn't going to steal jobs; it was going to help us do our jobs better, faster, and more creatively. It wasn't about replacing human connection, but enhancing how we communicate. It wasn't just a tool for today—it was a glimpse into the future.

The New World: A Future Powered by AI

Looking back, it's hard to imagine how we ever got by without ChatGPT. From personal assistance to customer service, education, and creativity, the AI has become a silent partner in countless industries. It didn't just make tasks easier—it fundamentally changed the way we think about work, learning, and even creativity.

ChatGPT's arrival wasn't a singular event. It was the beginning of an ongoing transformation. Every day, new applications, new uses, and new ideas are emerging. The AI is improving, adapting, and, most importantly, helping humanity move forward into a future that was once the realm of science fiction.

But the real question isn't how ChatGPT changed the world—it's how we, as a society, will continue to shape its role. With every conversation, every prompt, we are co-creating the future.

The launch of ChatGPT was just the start. What happens next is in our hands.

WHAT YOU'RE GOING TO LEARN FROM THIS BOOK

Welcome to a world where the impossible is no longer just a dream—it's already happening. Picture this: You type a few words, and suddenly, a machine generates an entire piece of art, writes a compelling blog post, or even solves a complex problem that's been bothering you for days. Sounds like something out of a sci-fi movie, right? But this is the reality we're stepping into. Welcome to the **future**. Welcome to the world of **Artificial Intelligence (AI)**, **Generative AI**, and **Prompt Engineering**.

In this book, you are about to embark on an exciting journey into the heart of AI technology—the very tools that are rapidly reshaping industries, creativity, and productivity at lightning speed. Whether you're a student, a business professional, or simply curious about how AI is transforming the world, what you're about to discover will change the way you view technology forever.

AI is no longer a buzzword; it's a driving force in our daily lives. From voice assistants like **Siri** and **Alexa** that listen to our commands, to **AI-powered cars** navigating the roads and even **AI-driven healthcare** systems diagnosing diseases, these intelligent systems are no longer just tools; they've become partners in our everyday tasks. But here's where it gets even more exciting: **Generative AI**. This technology doesn't just analyze data—it **creates**. It generates new ideas, new art, new solutions, and transforms creativity in ways that were once unimaginable.

Imagine this: You've been struggling to come up with a compelling pitch for your new startup. In the past, you might have spent hours brainstorming or hired someone to craft it for you. But now, with **Generative AI**, all you need to do is type a simple prompt like, "Write me a creative pitch for my innovative tech company," and within seconds, you have a polished draft that's engaging, relevant, and tailored to your needs. What's even more mind-blowing is that the machine doesn't just follow your instructions—it **builds upon your ideas**, improving them and taking them in directions you hadn't even considered.

So, how does this magic work? The answer lies in **Generative AI** and **Large Language Models (LLMs)**, like **GPT**. These models aren't just answering questions—they're thinking, creating, and innovating in ways we're only beginning to comprehend. They are the technology behind everything from chatbots and essay generators to music composition and even code creation. These models **don't just respond**; they **create** something new.

But here's the key to unlocking the full potential of these technologies: **Prompt Engineering**. This is where you come in. By learning how to craft the right prompts, you can unlock the true power of AI. Think of it as learning the perfect way to ask questions or give instructions to a hyper-intelligent assistant capable of doing anything—whether that's writing a novel, designing a website, or even planning your dream vacation.

As you turn the pages of this book, you will not only learn how these systems work but also discover how they can **transform your life**, **your business**, and **your creative projects**. This isn't just about using AI—it's about mastering it to enhance your efficiency, creativity, and innovation.

What's in store for you as you read on?

- The **fundamentals** of AI and how it's evolving to solve real-world problems.
- How **Generative AI** is changing the creative landscape by generating original content.
- The **art and science of Prompt Engineering**, where you'll learn how to communicate with AI to extract its full potential.
- **Real-world applications** of AI that are already transforming industries like healthcare, entertainment, business, and education.

By the end of this journey, you'll not only understand the immense power of AI but also know how to use it in ways you never thought possible. So, fasten your seatbelt—because we're diving headfirst into a world where creativity, innovation, and AI are seamlessly working together to shape the future.

Are you ready to explore the AI revolution? Let's dive in!

Introduction to AI and Generative AI

"AI is the new electricity. Just as electricity transformed industries a century ago, AI will reshape the world today."

- AI pioneer Andrew Ng

I
Welcome

Alright, let's start with something exciting. Imagine you're living in a world where machines aren't just tools but collaborators—creating art, solving problems, and even predicting your needs before you realize them. Sounds like science fiction, right? Well, **welcome to the Age of Artificial Intelligence.**

Let me explain how we got here. AI has evolved from being just a buzzword to the backbone of innovations we interact with daily. Think of Siri, Alexa, or Google Assistant—they're not just fancy gadgets; they're examples of how AI is simplifying our lives. Want to know tomorrow's weather or play your favorite song? Just ask them! But AI doesn't stop there—it's driving cars, detecting diseases, and even creating music and art. Cool, isn't it?

Now, let's zoom in on something even more fascinating: Generative AI. What does that mean? Basically, it's an AI that doesn't just analyze or recognize—it creates. Think about this: You give an AI a prompt, like "Write me a song in the style of Taylor Swift," and voila—it generates something brand new! That's generative AI in action. It's not just copying; it's creating something original, and the potential here is mind-blowing.

For instance, have you heard of GPT? It stands for Generative Pre-trained Transformer. Fancy name, I know. But all you need to know is that it's like the brain behind tools that can write essays, answer tricky questions, and even code. GPT-3 and 4, for example, is so advanced that it feels like you're chatting with a human. You could tell it, "Hey, write me a marketing pitch for my startup," and it'll churn out something impressive in seconds. Imagine the hours you save!

And here's the kicker: Generative AI isn't limited to text. It's designing virtual clothes, composing symphonies, and even editing films. Yes, you heard that right. AI tools like Runway AI are helping filmmakers cut scenes and add special effects without breaking a sweat. It's like having a super-efficient assistant that never sleeps.

Now, let's talk about the nuts and bolts. AI agents are another game-changer. Think of them as autonomous systems that make decisions, learn from their actions, and adapt over time. For example, those self-driving cars you see? They're powered by AI agents. They process data from sensors, figure out what's happening around them, and make split-second decisions—all without a human behind the wheel.

Companies like Waymo and Tesla are already rolling out these vehicles. Imagine a world where traffic jams are minimized, accidents are rare, and you can sit back and relax while your car drives you home. Elon Musk calls it a revolution that'll save lives—and I agree. We're not far from seeing this as the norm.

And what about healthcare? AI is a lifesaver—literally. It's diagnosing diseases earlier and more accurately than ever before. Take diabetic retinopathy, for instance. Google developed an AI that scans eye images and detects this condition with greater precision than doctors. It's not replacing doctors; it's making them superheroes. That's the power of AI.

But here's something even cooler: AI doesn't just help experts. It's here for everyone. Tools like Copy.ai make it easier for entrepreneurs to write ads, blog posts, or social media captions without hiring a professional. It's like having a creative partner who's always ready to brainstorm.

So, what's the big picture? AI isn't just about making life easier—it's about enhancing our creativity, productivity, and even our humanity. We're not replacing ourselves with machines; we're amplifying what we can do with them. The best part? This is just the beginning. We're stepping into a future where AI is as essential as electricity. And trust me, you'll want to be part of this journey.

II
What is Artificial Intelligence (AI)?

Welcome to the World of AI

Imagine this: You ask your phone to send a message, and it understands exactly what you mean and types it out for you. You use a voice assistant like Siri or Alexa, and it responds to your commands, telling you the weather, setting reminders, or even playing your favorite music. These actions are all powered by something called Artificial Intelligence (AI).

But what exactly is AI? How does it work, and why is it becoming such a big part of our everyday lives? Let's break it down together.

AI: A Simple Definition

At its core, Artificial Intelligence is the ability of machines or computers to perform tasks that typically require human intelligence. These tasks can range from simple activities like recognizing your voice to more complex processes like diagnosing diseases or even writing stories (like what we're doing here!).

AI is not a single technology but rather a collection of technologies that allow machines to think, learn, and make decisions based on the information they receive.

From Science Fiction to Reality

The idea of AI has been around for a long time. If you've ever watched movies like The Terminator or The Matrix, you've seen futuristic depictions of AI – machines that think for themselves and might even take over the world. While that makes for an exciting movie plot, the reality is much more grounded and helpful.

In today's world, AI is all around us. It's in your smartphone, in the recommendations you get on YouTube, in self-driving cars, and even in your email's spam filter. In fact, AI is already making our lives easier and more productive in many ways, often without us even noticing.

Key Concepts of AI

To understand how AI works, we need to look at a few basic ideas:

1. **Machine Learning (ML):** This is one of the most important aspects of AI. Imagine teaching a child to recognize animals. You show them pictures of a dog and say, "This is a dog." Over time, the child learns to identify dogs in other pictures on their own. Similarly, with machine learning, we feed a computer system lots of examples (data), and it learns patterns and makes predictions based on those examples.For instance, when you use Google search, it learns from your previous searches and starts to predict what you might be looking for next. The more data it gets, the better it gets at making predictions.

2. **Deep Learning:** This is a more advanced form of machine learning that uses artificial neural networks to mimic the way humans process information. Neural networks are inspired by the way the human brain works. Deep learning is particularly good at handling complex tasks, like recognizing faces in photos or understanding speech.

3. **Natural Language Processing (NLP):** Have you ever talked to Siri or used a translation app? That's NLP at work. It's the AI ability to understand, interpret, and respond to human language. NLP helps AI systems understand words, phrases, and even the context of a conversation.

4. **Computer Vision:** This allows machines to interpret and make sense of visual information. It's the technology behind things like facial recognition, self-driving cars, and even AI systems that can analyze medical images to detect diseases.

Types of AI

There are three main categories of AI that help us understand how smart or capable an AI system is:

1. **Narrow AI (Weak AI):** This is the most common type of AI today. Narrow AI is designed to do one specific task. For example, an AI program that can recommend songs based on your music preferences or a chatbot that helps answer customer service questions. Narrow AI doesn't "think" or "understand" like humans; it just performs the task it's been trained for.
2. **General AI (Strong AI):** This is the AI that you might see in science fiction. General AI would be able to understand, learn, and apply intelligence across a wide range of tasks, just like a human. It would have the ability to reason, solve problems, and make decisions in any situation. We don't have general AI yet, but researchers are working hard on it.
3. **Superintelligent AI:** This is a theoretical concept where AI surpasses human intelligence in every aspect—creativity, problem-solving, and emotional understanding. While it's exciting to imagine, superintelligent AI is still far off in the future.

How Does AI Learn?

You might be wondering, "How does AI actually learn all of this stuff?" Well, AI learns in a way that's somewhat similar to how we learn.

- **Training with Data:** AI systems are trained on massive amounts of data. For example, a facial recognition system is shown thousands of pictures of faces, and it learns to recognize patterns that help it identify who's in the picture. The more data the AI receives, the more accurate it becomes.
- **Feedback Loop:** Just like when we practice something and get better with feedback, AI improves over time with more data and corrections. If an AI makes a mistake, it learns from that mistake and adjusts its understanding.

Real-World Examples of AI

Now that we have a better understanding of AI, let's explore how it's used in the real world.

1. **Virtual Assistants:** Siri, Alexa, and Google Assistant are powered by AI. They listen to your voice, interpret your commands, and respond. They can set reminders, play music, answer questions, and much more.
2. **Healthcare:** AI is revolutionizing healthcare by helping doctors diagnose diseases more accurately. AI-powered tools analyze medical data, such as X-rays and MRIs, to detect problems like tumors or fractures.
3. **E-commerce and Recommendations:** If you've ever browsed Amazon and received recommendations like "Customers who bought this also bought," that's AI at work. It looks at your browsing history, compares it with other customers' patterns, and suggests products you might like.
4. **Self-Driving Cars:** Companies like Tesla are developing AI systems that can drive cars autonomously. These systems use computer vision, machine learning, and deep learning to interpret their surroundings, make decisions, and safely navigate the road.

The Future of AI

So, where is AI headed? The future of AI is full of exciting possibilities. As technology continues to improve, we can expect AI to become even more integrated into our lives. From healthcare to entertainment to how we work, AI will help us become more efficient, creative, and productive. But with these advancements come challenges, including ethical considerations, privacy concerns, and job displacement. These are important topics we'll explore later in this book.

> *"AI is no longer a futuristic concept; it's part of our everyday lives. Whether it's helping you find the best route to work, making your shopping experience easier, or enhancing your productivity at work, AI is here to stay. The more we learn about it, the better we can understand how it can work for us."*

III

What is Generative AI?

Hello Again! Let's Dive Into the World of Generative AI

Have you ever wondered how an app can generate an image from just a few words, or how a computer can write a poem or even a full-length article? Or maybe you've heard about AI creating music, paintings, or even realistic videos that seem like magic.

Welcome to the fascinating world of Generative AI!

Generative AI is a special kind of technology that's capable of creating new content—content that never existed before—just by learning from the data it's given. It's not just about understanding or recognizing patterns like regular AI, but about generating something original. Imagine having a machine that can be an artist, a writer, or even a composer—all powered by data and smart algorithms.

You don't have to be a tech expert to understand how it works. Let's walk through it together in simple terms.

What Exactly is Generative AI?

To put it simply, **Generative AI** refers to any type of AI system that can create something new. It could be anything from a picture, a poem, or even an entire song. It doesn't just look at data—it creates things based on what it has learned from large datasets.

Let's take a step back for a second. Imagine an artist. Before they create a painting, they spend time observing and studying other works of art. Over time, they start to understand what makes a good painting—colors, shapes, patterns, and emotions. Eventually, they create their own piece based on that knowledge.

Generative AI works similarly. It looks at tons of data—like books, images, or music—and learns patterns and structures. Once it has learned enough, it can start generating new things that resemble what it has been trained on, but with its own unique twist. The best part? The content it creates is often surprising, original, and sometimes even more creative than you might expect!

How Does Generative AI Work?

Now, let's look at how Generative AI actually learns and creates:

1. **Learning from Data:** Generative AI starts by looking at a massive amount of data. For example, if we want an AI to write a poem, we give it access to lots of poems and literature. The AI studies the structure, the language, and the rhythm of words. By doing this, it learns how poems are typically written. *Think of it like this: If you wanted to learn to write poems, you would read poems by great poets and practice. The more you read and practice, the better you become at it. Generative AI does the same thing, but at a much faster pace.*

2. **Generative Models:** To create something new, Generative AI uses generative models—these are the underlying algorithms that help the AI turn its learned knowledge into new content. One popular type of generative model is called Generative Adversarial Networks (GANs). Here's the fun part: Imagine there are two AI systems—one is trying to create something new, like a picture of a cat, and the other is trying to decide if it's a real cat or a fake one. These two AIs challenge each

other, which helps the AI learn to generate more realistic content over time.*Over time, this back-and-forth process makes the AI better at creating realistic images, text, or even music.*

3. **The Role of Neural Networks:** A neural network is like the brain of the AI. It's a system designed to process information, just like the human brain does. It takes the data, analyzes it, and finds patterns in it. Neural networks are the backbone of most AI technologies, including Generative AI, allowing the AI to make connections between different pieces of data and generate new ideas.

Generative AI in Action: Real-World Examples

Alright, so now you know how Generative AI works. But how is it actually being used? Let's look at some cool, real-world applications where Generative AI is already making waves:

1. **Text Generation:** Imagine you want to write a blog post, a short story, or even a poem, but you're struggling to get started. Generative AI can help you out. By simply giving it a prompt like, "Write a story about a detective solving a mysterious case," the AI can generate entire stories with different characters, settings, and twists. This technology is used by tools like GPT-4 (a language model) to generate human-like text. Not only can it generate coherent sentences, but it can also imitate specific writing styles. Want a story written like Shakespeare? The AI can do that!

2. **Image Creation:** If you've ever wanted to see an image of something you've only imagined, Generative AI can bring that to life. Tools like DALL-E and MidJourney allow users to describe anything—"a futuristic city on Mars," or "a dragon made of fire"—and the AI will generate an image of it.The beauty of this is that you don't need to be an artist to create beautiful, surreal, or imaginative images. The AI takes care of it for you.

3. **Music Composition:** Generative AI is also helping musicians create new music. AI tools like Amper Music and Suno Ai can compose original songs based on user preferences—be it a classical melody, a jazzy rhythm, or an electronic beat. You can even set the mood and the instruments, and the AI will generate a complete track. It's like having your own AI-powered composer!

4. **Video and Animation:** Ever heard of deepfake technology? While it can be controversial, it's an example of how Generative AI is being used to create realistic videos. AI can take a person's image and make them appear to say or do something they didn't actually do. While deepfakes have raised ethical concerns, the underlying technology is also being used for more positive purposes, like creating animations or producing special effects for films.

The Benefits of Generative AI

Now that we know what Generative AI is and how it works, let's talk about how it's benefiting society. Here are a few ways it's improving our daily lives:

1. **Fostering Creativity:** Generative AI is a great tool for creators. Artists, musicians, writers, and designers are using AI to help them brainstorm, experiment with new ideas, and complete their projects faster. It's like having a creative assistant who never runs out of ideas.
2. **Personalization:** Whether it's movies, music, or product recommendations, Generative AI helps personalize content for individuals. If you've ever felt like your favorite app knows exactly what you want, it's likely because of AI creating tailored suggestions based on your preferences.
3. **Making Learning Fun and Easy:** Generative AI is helping students and learners in creative ways. Imagine AI generating practice exercises in a foreign language or even providing you with interactive explanations for complex topics. It can adapt to the learner's needs and help them progress faster.
4. **Business Innovation:** In business, Generative AI is being used for product design, marketing materials, and even for generating new ideas that can lead to innovative breakthroughs. This is helping companies move faster, think outside the box, and stay competitive.

The Challenges and Ethical Considerations

Of course, with great power comes great responsibility. While Generative AI is amazing, it also comes with challenges and ethical considerations:

1. **Quality and Accuracy:** Sometimes, the content generated by AI might look or sound great at first glance, but it could still contain inaccuracies or errors. For instance, an AI-generated article might sound convincing but could be filled with misleading information. It's important to double-check and verify AI-generated content before using it.
2. **Deepfakes and Misinformation:** One of the biggest concerns with Generative AI is the potential for deepfakes, or realistic but fake videos, which could be used to spread misinformation. As this technology becomes more advanced, we need to be careful about how it is used and ensure that it is not used to deceive people.
3. **Who Owns the Content?:** If Generative AI creates a piece of artwork, a song, or a video, who owns it? Is it the person who trained the AI, the person who gave the prompt, or the AI itself? These are important legal and ethical questions that need to be addressed as AI continues to evolve.

The Future of Generative AI

Generative AI is only just beginning, and its potential is enormous. In the future, we can expect it to become even more sophisticated, creating more realistic and impactful content in every field. From entertainment and education to business and healthcare, Generative AI will be at the heart of innovation.

But remember—just like any powerful tool, we must use it responsibly and ethically. As we continue to explore this exciting technology, let's work together to harness its power for good.

IV

The Building Blocks of AI and Generative AI

Welcome to Chapter 3! Now that you've learned what AI and Generative AI can do, it's time to dive into how these technologies work. In this chapter, we'll break down the building blocks that power AI—step by step—so that you can understand how these systems learn, think, and even create new things. Don't worry, we're keeping it simple and fun, no technical jargon!

Data, Models, and Training in AI: The Foundation of Intelligence

Imagine you're teaching a child to identify a cat. You show them thousands of pictures of cats, and with each picture, you point out the key features: the pointy ears, the tail, the whiskers. After seeing enough pictures, the child begins to recognize a cat in any new image they come across, even if it looks slightly different from the ones they've seen before. AI works in a very similar way, learning from data to make decisions and predictions.

Here's how it breaks down:

- **Data:** Data is the fuel that powers AI. It's the raw information that AI uses to learn and make decisions. Just like a child needs lots of examples to learn something, AI needs a large amount of data to recognize patterns. In our cat example, the data would be thousands of pictures of cats labeled "cat" and "not cat."

- **Models:** A model is like the brain of the AI system. It's what helps AI make sense of the data. After seeing enough examples, the model learns to identify patterns—like recognizing what a cat looks like from various angles or in different environments.
- **Training:** This is the process of teaching AI by feeding it data. Think of it as homework: the more data the AI sees, the better it gets at understanding the task. The AI doesn't know everything upfront, but as it processes more data, it gradually gets better at making decisions or predictions. So, training is like getting the AI ready for a test—where it learns from all the data before it can apply its knowledge.

Neural Networks: The Brain Behind AI

You've probably heard of neural networks—but what exactly are they, and why are they so important in AI?

Imagine the human brain: billions of tiny neurons are connected and work together to help us think, recognize patterns, and make decisions. In AI, a neural network is a system of artificial neurons that are designed to mimic the way our brain works. These artificial neurons help the AI recognize patterns in data, make sense of complex information, and even create new things.

Here's how it works:

- **Neurons:** Just like your brain has neurons that process information, AI has artificial neurons that help it make decisions. These neurons are connected in layers, much like how neurons in the brain communicate.
- **Layers:** A neural network has multiple layers, each one helping the AI analyze data at a deeper level. The first layer might recognize basic shapes, while the next layer might recognize features like whiskers or ears, and so on. In the end, the AI can recognize an entire cat.
- **Learning Through Layers:** Neural networks are designed to process information in layers. The deeper the network (the more layers it has), the more sophisticated the learning process. Each layer helps the AI get better at understanding the data.

How Generative AI Works: Creativity Meets AI

In Generative AI, the goal isn't just to recognize things—it's to create something new. Just like an artist paints a picture or a writer pens a novel, Generative AI creates new content by learning from data. It uses the same building blocks we've discussed, but with a twist—it takes everything it's learned and creates something original.

Here's how Generative AI works:

- **Learning from Examples:** Just like an artist looks at thousands of paintings to develop their style, Generative AI learns from large amounts of data—whether that's text, images, music, or even videos. For instance, if you show a generative model thousands of paintings, it learns the different techniques, colors, and styles.
- **Creating New Content:** Once the AI has learned from these examples, it can generate something new. Let's say you want an AI to generate an image of a "cat playing the piano." The AI uses its understanding of cats and pianos from its training and combines them to generate a brand new image that has never been seen before.

Key Algorithms and Frameworks: The Brains Behind the Creativity

To make AI work, we need algorithms—step-by-step instructions that guide how the AI learns. These algorithms are like the recipes for AI's success, helping it learn from data and generate new, creative outputs. Let's take a look at some of the most powerful algorithms in Generative AI:

GPT-3 (Generative Pre-trained Transformer 4)

You've likely heard of GPT-4, the AI that can write essays, poetry, or even code. GPT-4 is a language model—meaning it's trained to understand and generate human language. Here's how it works:

- **Training:** GPT-4 has read billions of words from books, websites, and articles, which gives it a broad understanding of language.
- **Creativity:** When you give GPT-4 a prompt, like "Write a poem about the moon," it uses everything it has learned to generate text that is coherent and meaningful. It doesn't just repeat things—it creates something

entirely new based on the prompt.

BERT (Bidirectional Encoder Representations from Transformers)

While GPT-4 focuses on generating text, BERT is a model designed to understand language. The key to BERT is that it reads text both from left to right and right to left, helping it understand the context of words more effectively.

- Contextual Understanding: BERT helps machines understand the meaning behind sentences by looking at the surrounding words. For example, in the sentence "The cat chased the dog," BERT can recognize that "chased" is the verb and that "cat" is the subject, providing better understanding.

DALL-E (and DALL-E 3)

Imagine describing a picture and having AI create it instantly. That's exactly what DALL-E does! DALL-E is a Generative AI model that can turn text descriptions into images.

- **How It Works:** You could tell DALL-E, "Create an image of a purple elephant flying through the clouds," and DALL-E will generate that image for you, even if it's something completely fantastical.
- **Application:** DALL-E's power lies in its ability to create visual content from simple descriptions, making it a game-changer for industries like design, marketing, and entertainment.

Putting It All Together: Data, Models, Neural Networks, and Algorithms

Now that we've learned about the core components of AI, let's put it all together:

1. **Data** is the raw material—like pictures, text, or numbers—that AI uses to learn.
2. **Models** are the "brains" of AI, helping it make decisions and predictions based on data.
3. **Neural networks** are like the AI's processing unit, helping it recognize complex patterns and make sense of data.
4. **Algorithms** are the step-by-step instructions that guide the AI in learning and creating.

Together, these building blocks enable Generative AI to not only recognize patterns but also create new and innovative content, like generating text, images, and music.

V

The Rise and Evolution of AI and Generative AI

Welcome to Chapter 4! In the previous chapters, we laid the groundwork for understanding what AI and Generative AI are, and now it's time to explore their journey over time. We'll walk through the key milestones in AI's development, the driving forces behind its rise, and the groundbreaking breakthroughs that have shaped the AI landscape today. Whether you're tech-savvy or not, this chapter will guide you through the evolution of AI in a way that's simple and engaging.

Key Milestones in the Development of AI

AI's story is full of fascinating twists and turns. Let's take a step back and look at the pivotal moments in AI's evolution, which have led us to where we are today.

The Birth of AI (1950s - 1960s)

AI didn't appear out of nowhere—it was born from the curiosity and ingenuity of early thinkers who imagined a world where machines could think, learn, and adapt. Here's where it all began:

- **Alan Turing's Vision (1950):** In 1950, British mathematician Alan Turing published his seminal paper, "Computing Machinery and Intelligence," where he posed a simple yet profound question: Can machines think? This question laid the foundation for AI research and introduced the Turing Test, a method for measuring a machine's ability to exhibit intelligent behavior.

- The Dartmouth Conference (1956): In 1956, AI researchers, including John McCarthy and Marvin Minsky, gathered at Dartmouth College to formally coin the term "Artificial Intelligence." This was the birth of AI as a field of study, marking a significant step forward in the quest to build intelligent machines.

The First AI Winter (1970s)

Despite the excitement in the 1950s and 1960s, progress in AI faced significant challenges. Computers weren't powerful enough to handle complex tasks, and AI research began to slow down. This period is often referred to as the AI Winter.

- Researchers had high hopes but faced roadblocks, such as limited computing power and the inability of early AI systems to solve real-world problems. As a result, funding dried up, and AI research took a backseat.

The Resurgence of AI (1980s)

Despite the setbacks, AI wasn't done. In the 1980s, AI came roaring back with expert systems—software designed to emulate human expertise in specific areas.

- Expert Systems like MYCIN (a medical diagnostic tool) helped doctors diagnose diseases by mimicking the decision-making process of human experts. This showed the world that AI had real, practical applications, even if it wasn't yet the "thinking" machine people had dreamed of.

The Data Explosion and Machine Learning (1990s - 2000s)

As the internet boomed and computers became faster, AI found new opportunities. This was the era of Machine Learning (ML) and Big Data.

- **Machine Learning** enabled computers to learn from data rather than needing to be explicitly programmed. For instance, AI systems could now recognize speech, detect objects in images, and even predict trends based on past data.
- **Big Data**—the massive amounts of data generated by the internet, social media, and business transactions—gave AI the raw material it needed to improve its learning and decision-making. More data meant smarter, more accurate AI models.

The AI Revolution (2010s - Present)

The 2010s witnessed the true explosion of AI, with innovations that seemed straight out of science fiction. This period saw the birth of Deep Learning and Generative AI, technologies that reshaped what AI could do.

- **Deep Learning:** This is a form of Neural Networks that uses many layers of interconnected nodes to learn complex patterns. Deep Learning allowed AI to do things that were once unimaginable, like recognizing speech with near-human accuracy, understanding images, and playing complex games like Go and Chess.
- **Generative AI:** This is the next frontier of AI—machines that can create new content. From text generation (like GPT-4) to image creation (like DALL-E), Generative AI models are capable of creating new ideas, artwork, music, and even entire essays with little more than a few instructions. These breakthroughs opened up new possibilities for AI, allowing it to go beyond being just a tool to one that can generate new things.

The Role of Data and Computing Power in AI's Evolution

As we saw, AI's growth wouldn't have been possible without two key ingredients: Data and Computing Power. Let's break down how these elements have been pivotal in pushing AI forward.

The Data Revolution

Data is the fuel that powers AI. Think of it like food for the brain. The more data AI has, the better it gets at learning, making decisions, and predicting outcomes.

- **Early AI** didn't have access to much data, so it struggled to make accurate predictions. But with the advent of the internet, data became abundant. Now, AI has access to billions of data points—from social media posts to online transactions and even sensor data from devices.
- **Big Data** has been a game-changer because it allows AI to learn from vast amounts of information. For example, if you want to teach an AI system to recognize pictures of cats, it needs access to millions of photos of cats. The more examples it sees, the better it can recognize a cat in any photo.

Computing Power: The Accelerator

But data alone isn't enough. AI also needs powerful computers to process all that information. Early computers didn't have the capability to handle large-scale AI tasks, but with the rise of Graphics Processing Units (GPUs) and Cloud Computing, things changed dramatically.

- **GPUs**—originally designed for gaming—are perfect for running AI models because they can process multiple calculations at once. This is critical for tasks like image recognition, where AI must analyze and process large amounts of visual data.
- **Cloud Computing** allowed AI to scale its operations, using the computing power of multiple machines at once. This meant that AI models could train faster and more efficiently, opening the door to more complex applications and real-time decision-making.

Thanks to the combination of big data and supercharged computing, AI has been able to advance at an unprecedented rate.

The Impact of Breakthroughs Like Deep Learning and Reinforcement Learning

Two of the most important breakthroughs that shaped modern AI are Deep Learning and Reinforcement Learning. Let's take a closer look at how these innovations changed the game.

Deep Learning: Making AI Smarter

Deep Learning refers to a class of algorithms that uses multiple layers of neural networks to analyze and learn from data. These layers help the AI system understand more complex patterns in data.

- Imagine teaching an AI to recognize a dog in a photo. The first layer might detect edges, the second layer might detect shapes, and the third might recognize that those shapes form the outline of a dog. By stacking more layers, Deep Learning allows AI to understand much more intricate details and make better predictions.
- Deep Learning has powered breakthroughs in speech recognition, image recognition, and natural language processing. For example, voice assistants like Siri or Alexa rely on deep learning to understand and respond to human speech.

Reinforcement Learning: Teaching AI by Rewarding It

Another major breakthrough is Reinforcement Learning (RL), which is a type of learning where AI learns by interacting with its environment and receiving feedback. Think of it like teaching a dog a trick by rewarding it with treats when it gets it right.

- In Reinforcement Learning, the AI system tries out different actions and learns from the rewards or punishments it receives. This is particularly useful for tasks like playing video games, controlling robots, or making decisions in real-time.
- RL is what enables AI to optimize decisions in dynamic environments. For instance, self-driving cars use RL to navigate traffic, avoid obstacles, and make driving decisions.

Mastering Prompt Engineering

""Those who know how to prompt the AI to do their bidding and to do it faster and better and more creatively than anyone else is going to be golden. The AI whisperers will soon be very much in demand. In a world filled with uncertainty, where we are all seeking answers, ironically asking the right questions is going to be the next superpower.""

VI

The Dawn of a New Era in Human-Computer Interaction

For decades, programming languages like Python, Java, and C++ have been the primary tools for instructing computers to perform tasks. These languages, though powerful, require expertise and a steep learning curve. They act as bridges between human intent and machine execution but are inherently technical and demanding to learn. Now, with the advent of generative AI, a revolutionary shift is taking place—prompts are emerging as the new "language" for interacting with machines.

Imagine you're an artist, not trained in coding, but you want to create a digital painting. Instead of learning how to write complex algorithms, you can now instruct an AI like DALL-E by simply describing your vision:

"Create an image of a serene village in Kerala with coconut trees, backwaters, and a houseboat during sunset."

This single sentence is your "code." It directs the AI to execute your idea, bypassing traditional programming entirely.

Prompts are not just a tool—they are a paradigm shift, democratizing access to AI and enabling anyone, regardless of technical expertise, to harness its power.

What is a Prompt?

At its core, a prompt is a natural language instruction given to an AI model, guiding it to perform a task. Think of a prompt as a conversation starter or a detailed request to the AI. Unlike programming, where you must follow rigid syntax rules, prompting uses plain, everyday language. This makes it accessible to anyone who can articulate their thoughts clearly.

Prompts can be as simple as:

- "Summarize this article in two sentences."

Or as complex as:

- "Generate a step-by-step guide for starting a small-scale organic farming business in India, including initial investment, potential crops, and expected returns."

How Prompts Resemble Programming Code

Prompts and traditional code share a fundamental similarity: both provide a set of instructions to a machine to perform a task. However, they differ in their form and complexity:

Aspect	Traditional Programming	Prompts
Syntax	Requires strict syntax and formatting.	Uses natural language, no syntax needed.
Audience	Designed for programmers and developers.	Accessible to everyone.
Learning Curve	High; requires understanding of logic, algorithms, and frameworks.	Low; requires clarity in communication.
Execution	Requires coding, debugging, and testing.	Immediate; interpreted by AI directly.
Output Generation	Code is written to generate specific outputs or perform computations.	Prompts guide AI to produce creative, informative, or functional outputs.

Programming vs Promts

Why Prompts Are the New Programming Language

1. **Accessibility:**In India, millions of students, entrepreneurs, and small-business owners face barriers in learning traditional programming. With prompts, these barriers vanish. Imagine a farmer in rural Maharashtra using a generative AI app to optimize crop rotation schedules by simply typing a question "Which crops should I grow after wheat to improve soil fertility?"

2. **Speed and Efficiency:**Writing hundreds of lines of code to perform a task is time-consuming. With prompts, you can achieve the same result in seconds. For example:

   - **Code Task:** Writing Python code to analyze sales data.
   - **Prompt:** "Analyze this sales data and highlight the best-performing product categories in the last quarter."
   - **Result:** The AI delivers actionable insights instantly.

3. **Creativity and Flexibility:** Prompts unlock creativity in ways traditional coding cannot.

   - **Code Example:** Generating a pie chart using a library like Matplotlib.
   - **Prompt Example:** "Create a visually stunning infographic about India's population distribution by state."

4. **Language Diversity:** In a multilingual country like India, generative AI models trained in regional languages make it possible to use prompts in Hindi, Tamil, Bengali, or Telugu.

5. **Democratizing AI:** Prompts empower individuals who don't have access to formal education or advanced technical skills to solve problems. A shopkeeper in Jaipur can use an AI-powered assistant with prompts to create invoices, track inventory, or plan marketing campaigns.

Examples: Prompting as Programming

To illustrate how prompts act as the new programming language, let's explore a few real-world scenarios:

1. **Content Creation:**

   - **Old Way:** Hiring a content writer or learning to write yourself.
   - **With Prompts:** "Write a 500-word blog on how yoga can reduce stress, using examples from Indian practices."

2. **Data Analysis:**

   - **Old Way:** Writing SQL queries to extract insights.
   - **With Prompts:** "Analyze this CSV file of monthly expenses and identify trends in utility bills."

3. **Learning and Education:**

   - **Old Way:** Searching through textbooks or coding solutions.
   - **With Prompts:** "Explain the concept of zero from Indian mathematician Aryabhata's perspective."

4. **Art and Design:**

   - Old Way: Using graphic design software.
   - With Prompts: "Create an illustration of a Rangoli pattern inspired by Diwali celebrations."

Challenges and Opportunities

While prompts are revolutionary, they come with their own challenges:

- **Ambiguity:** A poorly structured prompt may lead to irrelevant results.
- **Bias:** If the AI model is trained on biased data, the outputs may reflect those biases.
- **Skillful Prompting:** Crafting effective prompts is a skill that requires practice and understanding of how AI models interpret input.

On the flip side, the opportunities are immense. India, with its vast diversity and unique needs, is poised to benefit greatly from this shift.

"*In the world of generative AI, prompts are more than just instructions—they are the new universal language for communication with machines. They democratize technology, making it accessible to a chaiwala in Lucknow, a student in Bengaluru, a small business owner in Coimbatore, or a tech enthusiast in Hyderabad, the bustling hub of India's AI and innovation ecosystem.*

As we move forward, mastering the art of prompting will be as essential as learning basic literacy. It is not just a skill but a gateway to unlocking the full potential of AI, empowering individuals, businesses, and communities across India."

VII
Unlocking AI's Potential

"*Imagine standing in the middle of a bustling Indian bazaar, like Chandni Chowk in Delhi or Charminar in Hyderabad. You need a specific item—a handcrafted wooden toy. If you vaguely ask shopkeepers for "something interesting," they might show you jewelry, clothes, or even spices. But if you clearly say, "I'm looking for a hand-carved wooden toy elephant made in Saharanpur," the response will be precise, saving you time and effort.*

*This analogy helps us understand what prompts do in generative AI. A **prompt** is the input you provide to the AI model—like your query to the shopkeeper—and the AI generates a response based on how well you've articulated your need. The better your prompt, the more relevant and useful the output will be.*"

Why Prompts Matter in Generative AI

In a diverse and complex country like India, clarity is essential to navigate the multitude of languages, cultures, and contexts. Prompts serve as the bridge between your intent and the AI's response, helping it cater to your needs effectively. Here's why they're so crucial:

1. **Setting Context**:
   India is a land of contrasts. Asking AI, "What's the weather today?" could lead to confusion. A more specific prompt like "What's the weather in

Jaipur today?" provides context, ensuring an accurate response tailored to your location.

2. **Ensuring Relevance**:
Without clarity, AI might provide irrelevant results.

   ○ **Example**:

      ▪ Prompt: "Recommend a good dish."

         ▪ AI Output: A generic response like "Try pasta or pizza."

      ▪ Better Prompt: "Recommend a popular vegetarian dish from South India."

         ▪ AI Output: "Masala dosa with coconut chutney and sambar."

3. **Unlocking Creativity**:
Well-structured prompts can inspire creative and culturally relevant responses.

   ○ **Example**:

      ▪ Prompt: "Write a poem about the Taj Mahal in the style of Rabindranath Tagore."
      ▪ Output: A beautifully crafted poem blending India's cultural and artistic heritage.

How Prompts Guide AI

AI models like ChatGPT, DALL-E, and others work by predicting patterns and generating outputs based on your input. Your prompt serves as the starting point for this prediction process. In an Indian context, prompts can be tailored to capture the rich diversity and complexity of our lives.

1. **Contextual Guidance**:
Just like a Bollywood director giving instructions to actors, prompts guide AI to set the stage for a task.

- ○ **Example**:

  - Basic Prompt: "Explain yoga."

    - AI Output: A general definition.

  - Refined Prompt: "Explain the history and benefits of yoga as practiced in India, with examples of key poses like Surya Namaskar."

    - AI Output: A culturally enriched response highlighting yoga's Indian roots.

2. **Cultural Relevance**:
   AI can produce outputs that reflect India's unique cultural identity.

   - ○ **Example**:

     - Prompt: "Generate a 5-day travel itinerary for a family visiting Rajasthan."
     - Output: A detailed itinerary including Jaipur, Udaipur, Jodhpur, and local experiences like camel rides and folk dances.

3. **Output Formatting**:
   Prompts can dictate how the output should look.

   - ○ **Example**:

     - Prompt: "List five Indian festivals celebrated across different states and describe their cultural significance."
     - Output: A neatly organized list (e.g., Diwali, Holi, Pongal, Onam, Durga Puja).

Examples of Effective Prompts

Here are real-world examples of how prompts can be tailored for Indian users:

1. **Text Generation with GPT-3**:

   - **Basic Prompt**: "Write about India's freedom struggle."

     - Output: A generic paragraph.

   - **Detailed Prompt**: "Write a 500-word essay about the role of Mahatma Gandhi in India's freedom struggle, focusing on non-violent resistance and key movements like the Dandi March."

     - Output: A detailed and insightful essay.

2. **Image Generation with DALL-E**:

   - **Basic Prompt**: "A painting of a festival."

     - Output: A generic festival scene.

   - **Detailed Prompt**: "A digital painting of an Indian family celebrating Diwali, lighting diyas, and bursting crackers against a backdrop of a decorated home."

     - Output: A culturally specific and vibrant image.

3. **Code Generation with Codex**:

   - **Basic Prompt**: "Write Python code for calculating income tax."

     - Output: Generic tax calculation code.

   - **Detailed Prompt**: "Write Python code to calculate income tax in India for the financial year 2024-25, based on the new tax regime slabs."

     - Output: Contextually relevant code.

4. **Conversational AI**:

   - **Basic Prompt**: "Recommend a movie."

- Output: A random movie suggestion.

- **Detailed Prompt**: "Recommend a Bollywood movie from the 2000s that is family-friendly and features Shah Rukh Khan."

  - Output: A specific suggestion like *Kabhi Khushi Kabhie Gham*.

Advanced Prompting for Indian Users

To get the best results, prompts can be crafted with a deeper understanding of India's diversity:

1. **Instruction-Based Prompts**:

   - Example: "Summarize the Bhagavad Gita's teachings on karma in simple terms for a beginner."

2. **Role-Based Prompts**:

   - Example: "Act as a career counselor and recommend the best engineering colleges in India for computer science."

3. **Cultural Creativity Prompts**:

   - Example: "Write a folk tale set in rural Punjab about a farmer who discovers a magical well."

4. **Layered Prompts**:

   - Example: "Create a step-by-step guide for making biryani, followed by a brief history of its origins in India."

   "*India, with its vast cultural and linguistic diversity, offers an incredible playground for exploring the potential of generative AI. Prompts are your tools to ensure that AI understands and aligns with your needs, whether you're seeking historical knowledge, creative outputs, or practical solutions."*

VIII
Crafting Effective and Advanced Prompts

"In the vast landscape of generative AI, prompts are the bridge between human intent and machine response. Think of a prompt as the question you ask in a conversation or the instruction you give to a chef. The clearer and more precise your input, the closer the output aligns with your expectations. This chapter is dedicated to unraveling the art and science behind crafting prompts—from the basics to advanced techniques—so you can make AI work for you."

What Makes a Good Prompt?

A good prompt has three essential components: **clarity**, **specificity**, and **context.**

1. **Clarity:**
   Ambiguity is the enemy of a good response. If your prompt is vague, the AI's output may not meet your needs. A clear prompt leaves little room for misinterpretation.

   - Example: Instead of asking, *"Tell me about Hyderabad,"* you could say, *"Provide a historical overview of Hyderabad, focusing on its role in India's tech industry."*

2. **Specificity:**
The more specific you are, the better the results. AI thrives on detailed instructions.

   - Example: Compare *"Explain cloud computing"* with *"Explain cloud computing in simple terms for a 12-year-old student."*

3. **Context:**
Providing context ensures the AI understands the purpose and audience of your query.

   - Example: *"Summarize the novel 'Malgudi Days' as a study guide for high school students preparing for exams."*

Techniques for Crafting Prompts

Crafting prompts is an iterative process that involves experimentation. Let's explore techniques to create both simple and complex prompts effectively:

1. Start with the End Goal
Begin by identifying what you want the AI to deliver. Imagine you're asking a friend for help—what exactly do you want them to do?

- Example: If your goal is to write a blog, a prompt like *"Draft a 500-word blog about the benefits of organic farming in India"* sets clear expectations.

2. Use Role-Based Instructions
Assign a role to the AI to guide its tone, style, and content.

- Example: *"Act as a historian and write an account of Hyderabad's architectural evolution."*
This technique works well for tasks like professional writing, technical explanations, or creative storytelling.

3. Include Constraints or Formats
Constraints help in structuring the output.

- Example: *"Create a bulleted list of 10 points explaining the impact of AI in the Indian healthcare sector."*
- Example: *"Write a dialogue between two friends discussing how Hyderabad became a global tech hub."*

4. Iterative Refinement

AI doesn't always get it right on the first try. Start simple and refine based on the output.

- Initial Prompt: *"Explain renewable energy."*
- Refined Prompt: *"Explain the different types of renewable energy sources and their applications in rural India."*

5. Layering Complexity

For advanced prompts, combine multiple instructions:

- Example: *"Summarize the book 'The White Tiger' in 300 words, focusing on themes of class struggle, and include two quotes from the protagonist."*

Case Studies: Practical Examples of Effective Prompts

Case Study 1: Writing a Resume

- **Objective:** Create a professional resume for a fresh graduate in computer science.
- **Prompt:** *"Write a professional resume for a recent computer science graduate from Osmania University, Hyderabad, including a strong objective, skills section, and relevant project experience."*
- **Result:** A well-organized resume tailored to the tech industry.

Case Study 2: Generating Marketing Content

- **Objective:** Write a catchy tagline for a food delivery app.
- **Prompt:** *"Suggest a catchy tagline for a food delivery app based in Hyderabad that focuses on delivering biryani and other local delicacies."*
- **Result:** *"Biryani to Your Doorstep: Savor Hyderabad's Flavors in Minutes!"*

Case Study 3: Answering Complex Questions

- **Objective:** Explain a scientific concept simply.
- **Prompt:** *"Explain the concept of photosynthesis in a way that a 10-year-old in Hyderabad can understand."*
- **Result:** A clear and engaging explanation with relatable examples.

Refining Prompts for Better Results

Sometimes, your initial prompt may not produce the desired output. Here's how you can refine it:

1. **Identify the Gap:**
   Look at the response and determine what's missing or incorrect.

   - Example: If you wanted detailed information but received a generic answer, include phrases like *"in detail"* or *"with examples."*

2. **Add Constraints:**
   Tighten the scope to avoid irrelevant information.

   - Original Prompt: *"Tell me about AI in India."*
   - Refined Prompt: *"Provide an overview of AI startups in Hyderabad, focusing on healthcare and education."*

3. **Experiment with Formats:**
   Change how you ask the question to get different perspectives.

   - Example: Ask for a comparison: *"Compare the growth of AI industries in Bengaluru and Hyderabad over the last decade."*

The Indian Context of Prompt Engineering

Prompts can be tailored to suit diverse contexts, including India's unique needs and challenges:

- **Education:**
  "Create a study plan for an Indian student preparing for competitive exams using AI-powered tools."
- **Business:**
  "Draft an email introducing a new AI service for small businesses in Hyderabad."
- **Culture:**
  "Generate a script for a YouTube video discussing AI's role in preserving Indian classical music."

Mastering the Art of Prompt Crafting

To truly master prompting, practice is key. Here's a checklist for crafting great prompts:

1. Is your intent clear?
2. Have you specified your audience or purpose?
3. Does the prompt provide enough context or constraints?
4. Have you considered multiple approaches to framing your query?

> *"Prompts are not static—they evolve with your understanding of AI and the task at hand. By practicing these techniques and tailoring them to your needs, you'll unlock AI's potential to be a powerful assistant in every sphere of life."*

IX

Prompt Engineering Techniques: From Beginner to Advanced

"As the language of interaction with generative AI, prompts require more than just basic understanding; they demand skillful engineering. This chapter is your guide to mastering prompt engineering, starting with foundational techniques and progressing to advanced methods. Whether you're a beginner exploring AI or an advanced user optimizing workflows, these techniques will help you get the most from your AI interactions."

Why Prompt Engineering Matters

Before diving into techniques, let's understand the value of prompt engineering:

- **Precision:** The right prompt reduces irrelevant or inaccurate outputs.
- **Efficiency:** A well-structured prompt saves time by minimizing iterations.
- **Control:** Thoughtful prompts guide AI to provide tailored results, enhancing its usefulness across applications.

For example, an educational institute in Hyderabad might want AI to design a curriculum. A vague prompt like *"Create a syllabus for AI"* could lead to generic results, while a detailed prompt such as *"Design a 6-month AI syllabus for beginners, focusing on machine learning and practical applications in India"* delivers actionable output.

Foundations of Prompt Engineering

1. Structuring Your Prompt

Think of a prompt as a conversation starter that sets expectations. A well-structured prompt includes:

- **Role/Context:** Define the AI's role.
  Example: "You are a language tutor…"
- **Task/Goal:** Specify what you want.
  Example: "…who simplifies complex scientific concepts…"
- **Constraints/Format:** Provide guidelines or limitations.
  Example: "…in under 300 words using simple language."*

Template:
"You are [role]. Your task is to [goal] while [constraints]."

2. Using Active Language

AI responds better to direct and action-oriented instructions.

- Instead of: *"Can you explain?"*
- Use: *"Explain clearly in bullet points…"*

3. Iterative Refinement

Start simple and refine your prompt based on the output.

- **Initial Prompt:** "Write about AI's impact on jobs."
- **Refined Prompt:** "Write a 500-word essay discussing the impact of AI on jobs in India, highlighting both opportunities and challenges."

Intermediate Techniques for Prompt Engineering

4. Contextual Layering

Provide background information for nuanced responses.

- Example: *"You are an economist analyzing India's growth. Write a report on the role of AI in Hyderabad's tech industry, focusing on startups and job creation."*

5. Chained Prompts

Break complex tasks into smaller parts.

- Prompt 1: *"List the top AI startups in Hyderabad."*
- Prompt 2: *"For each startup, describe their main product and impact on local industries."*

This chaining method allows for deeper analysis and structured responses.

6. Experimenting with Creativity Modes

AI can shift between being factual, persuasive, or creative depending on your instruction.

- Factual: *"Provide a summary of the AI policy in India."*
- Persuasive: *"Write an article arguing for greater AI adoption in Indian agriculture."*
- Creative: *"Write a fictional story about an AI revolution in Hyderabad in 2030."*

7. Prompting for Specific Outputs

Specify the output format to streamline results.

- *"Summarize the impact of AI on Indian education in 5 bullet points."*
- *"Create a table comparing AI applications in healthcare and finance in India."*

Advanced Techniques for Prompt Engineering

8. Prompt Tuning

Fine-tune prompts for repetitive tasks or niche applications.

- **Scenario:** A logistics company in Hyderabad needs AI-generated delivery route optimizations.

    - Basic Prompt: *"Suggest efficient delivery routes for Hyderabad."*
    - Tuned Prompt: *"Suggest 3 efficient delivery routes for Hyderabad, prioritizing areas with high traffic density during peak hours."*

9. Leveraging System Messages

In advanced AI systems, you can use system messages to influence behavior.

- Example: *"You are an expert AI tutor. Be concise, avoid jargon, and focus on practical examples while answering."*

10. Multi-Layered Prompts

Combine multiple goals into a single, comprehensive prompt.

- Example: *"Write a 500-word essay on AI's impact on rural India, include statistics, provide 3 real-world examples, and conclude with potential challenges."*

11. Iterative Optimization

When a prompt doesn't work as expected, analyze and adjust:

- Add Constraints: *"Include statistics from Indian government reports."*
- Adjust Tone: *"Write for a school audience, keeping it simple and engaging."*
- Refine Focus: *"Focus on Hyderabad's pharmaceutical sector."*

Case Studies: Advanced Prompt Engineering in Action

Case Study 1: AI in Indian Agriculture

- **Objective:** Write a report on AI applications in Indian agriculture.
- **Initial Prompt:** *"Write about AI in agriculture."*
- **Refined Prompt:** *"Draft a 1000-word report on AI's impact on agriculture in India, focusing on crop yield improvement and weather prediction technologies. Include examples from Telangana and Karnataka."*

Case Study 2: Marketing Campaign for a Hyderabad-Based Startup

- **Objective:** Generate a marketing tagline for a local AI startup.
- **Prompt:***"Create a catchy tagline for an AI startup in Hyderabad specializing in healthcare innovations."*
- **Output:***"Caring Smarter: Hyderabad's AI Revolution in Healthcare!"*

Case Study 3: Educational Video Script

- **Objective:** Develop an engaging script for an educational YouTube video.
- **Prompt:***"Write a 2-minute script explaining how AI is shaping Hyderabad's tech landscape, with a focus on job creation and startup growth."*

Tips for Mastery

1. **Practice Regularly:** Experiment with different styles, formats, and complexities.
2. **Think Like a Programmer:** Approach prompts logically, breaking tasks into smaller steps.
3. **Stay Updated:** AI evolves rapidly; keep exploring new use cases and capabilities.
4. **Tailor for Context:** Align prompts with specific needs—whether for education, business, or creativity.

"The Role of Prompt Engineering in India's AI Journey

India, with its diverse needs and growing technological landscape, stands to benefit immensely from effective prompt engineering. Whether it's a student in Hyderabad optimizing their study routine, a farmer in rural Telangana using AI for weather insights, or an entrepreneur crafting marketing strategies, prompts are the key to unleashing AI's potential.

Mastering prompt engineering isn't just a technical skill—it's a transformative tool for empowerment and innovation."

X

Prompting Techniques: Unlocking AI's Full Potential

"*In the world of generative AI, the way you ask a question (or give a command) determines the kind of response you get. This is where prompting techniques come into play. They are like the secret recipes to get the most out of AI, whether you're chatting with a virtual assistant, designing marketing content, or solving complex problems.*

In this chapter, we'll explore prompting techniques in detail, breaking them down into simple, practical concepts. Let's take this journey step by step, with relatable examples and a conversational tone that feels like you're learning from a friend."

Why Do Prompting Techniques Matter?

Imagine you're in Hyderabad, standing at the Charminar, and you want directions to the nearest biryani spot. You could ask:

1. "Where's biryani?"
2. "Can you recommend a biryani place nearby?"
3. "What's the best-rated biryani restaurant within 5 km from here?"

Each version gets you a different type of answer. The first one is too vague, the second gets a broader response, and the third is specific and actionable. Prompting techniques are about crafting that third question—precise, clear, and designed to get the best results.

The Core Prompting Techniques

1. Zero-Shot Prompting

This is the simplest technique where you ask a question or give a command without providing examples.

Example:

- You: "Explain why Hyderabad is known as Cyberabad."
- AI: "Hyderabad is called Cyberabad due to its thriving IT and software industry, which includes tech hubs like HITEC City and numerous multinational companies."

When to Use:

- When the task is straightforward.
- When you don't need to guide AI with examples.

Tip: Keep your zero-shot prompts clear and focused to avoid vague responses.

2. One-Shot Prompting

Here, you provide one example to guide the AI.

Example:

You: "Write a formal email. For example: 'Dear Sir/Madam, I am writing to inform you about...'. Now, write an email about applying for leave."

AI: "Dear Manager, I am writing to formally request leave from December 20th to December 30th due to personal reasons..."

When to Use:

- When you want to set a tone or format.

- When a single example can clarify your expectations.

⁎

3. Few-Shot Prompting

This involves giving multiple examples to guide AI on the type of response you want.

Example:

You: "Here's how I want answers:

1. Hyderabad is known for its history. Example: 'The Charminar, built in 1591, is a historic landmark.'
2. Hyderabad is known for its food. Example: 'The city is famous for Hyderabadi biryani, a delicious rice dish.'
   Now, write about Hyderabad's tech industry."
   AI: "Hyderabad is known for its thriving tech industry. Example: 'The HITEC City, a technology hub, hosts many multinational companies like Microsoft and Google.'"

When to Use:

- For complex tasks that require specific styles or formats.
- When consistency in output is important.

⁎

Advanced Techniques: Taking Prompts to the Next Level

4. Chain-of-Thought Prompting

This technique encourages AI to "think aloud" by explaining its reasoning step by step.

Example:

You: "Why is Hyderabad a great place for startups? Think step by step."
AI:

1. "Hyderabad offers affordable office spaces compared to cities like Bengaluru."

2. "The city has a growing talent pool, thanks to prestigious institutions like IIT Hyderabad and IIIT Hyderabad."
3. "It provides strong government support through initiatives like T-Hub."
4. "The city's strategic location connects northern and southern India, making it ideal for businesses."

When to Use:

- For problem-solving or decision-making tasks.
- When you want to understand the reasoning behind an answer.

5. Instruction-Based Prompting

Here, you explicitly tell AI how to behave or what structure to follow.

Example:

You: "Summarize this paragraph in 3 bullet points:
'Hyderabad's IT industry has seen exponential growth over the past decade. With tech parks like HITEC City, it has attracted global giants such as Google, Amazon, and Facebook. The city's infrastructure and skilled workforce make it a preferred destination for tech investments.'"

AI:

- Hyderabad's IT industry has grown rapidly over the past decade.
- HITEC City has attracted companies like Google, Amazon, and Facebook.
- Strong infrastructure and talent make it ideal for tech investments.

When to Use:

- For tasks requiring structured outputs.
- When you need clarity and precision.

6. Iterative Refinement

This involves adjusting and improving your prompts based on the initial output.

Example:
You: "Write about Hyderabad's role in the pharmaceutical industry."
AI (First Attempt): "Hyderabad has a pharmaceutical industry."
You: "Expand on this. Mention leading companies, government initiatives, and its nickname as 'Genome Valley.'"
AI (Refined Response): "Hyderabad, often called 'Genome Valley,' is a hub for the pharmaceutical industry. Companies like Dr. Reddy's Laboratories and Bharat Biotech operate here. Government initiatives have further boosted its prominence in biotechnology and healthcare research."

When to Use:

- For fine-tuning responses.
- To extract deeper insights.

ॐ

Practical Applications in the Indian Context

1. Education
A teacher in Bengaluru can use AI to create lesson plans:
Prompt: *"Design a one-hour lesson plan on Indian independence for 10th-grade students, including activities and key discussion points."*

2. Business
A Hyderabad-based entrepreneur can use AI to draft a business proposal:
Prompt: *"Write a proposal for an e-commerce platform focusing on rural Telangana, highlighting logistics solutions and local employment opportunities."*

3. Daily Life
A homemaker in Coimbatore can get meal plans from AI:
Prompt: *"Suggest a vegetarian meal plan for a week using South Indian ingredients."*

Common Challenges and Solutions

Challenge 1: Vague Outputs

- **Problem:** You asked, "Tell me about Hyderabad," and got a generic response.

- **Solution:** Add specifics: "Write a 500-word essay on Hyderabad's historical landmarks and their significance."

Challenge 2: Overloaded Prompts

- **Problem:** You asked, "Write about Hyderabad's history, culture, economy, and tech growth," and got a scattered response.
- **Solution:** Split into smaller tasks:

1. "Write about Hyderabad's history and culture."
2. "Explain its economy and tech growth."

> "Prompting techniques are the foundation of effective AI interactions. Whether you're in a bustling city like Hyderabad or a quiet village in Kerala, mastering these techniques can empower you to achieve more with AI.
>
> The beauty of generative AI lies in its adaptability—it can be your tutor, your assistant, or even your storyteller. But like any relationship, the quality of your interaction depends on how you communicate. With the right prompting techniques, you're not just using AI; you're unlocking its true potential."

Demystifying Large Language Models (LLMs)

"

"Imagine a world where your thoughts are transformed into content, your ideas into solutions, and your questions into answers—LLMs make this future a reality."
Explanation: LLMs streamline many activities, from simplifying content creation to assisting businesses in automating responses. They act as intelligent tools to enhance productivity.

"

XI

What Are Large Language Models (LLMs)?

What Are LLMs?

Imagine you're talking to a chatbot on your phone, asking it questions, and it responds in a way that feels like you're chatting with a person. It can help you order food, write a message, or even tell you a joke. But what if this chatbot could also write essays, help you with your homework, and even draft business proposals? Well, that's exactly what **Large Language Models** (LLMs) can do—and much more.

In simple terms, an LLM is an advanced form of AI (Artificial Intelligence) that is specifically designed to understand and generate human-like text. Think of it as a highly intelligent assistant that can read, understand, and respond in a way that feels natural and intuitive. Whether it's answering your questions, writing a report, or even generating poetry, LLMs are capable of doing all of that by processing vast amounts of text data they've been trained on.

To put it in perspective, just like humans learn language by reading books, listening to conversations, and experiencing the world, LLMs are trained by being fed enormous amounts of text. This training helps the AI understand grammar, facts, nuances of language, and even complex topics, enabling it to converse with us intelligently.

Why Are LLMs Significant in AI?

LLMs are crucial to the advancement of Artificial Intelligence because they are one of the most powerful tools when it comes to language-related tasks. Previously, machines struggled to understand human language in a way that felt natural. Early AI systems would either misunderstand complex sentences or provide irrelevant responses. But with LLMs, AI has evolved to a point where it can now engage in detailed, context-aware conversations, answer questions accurately, write creatively, and even solve complex problems.

What makes LLMs special is their **ability to learn**. Instead of being explicitly programmed with specific answers, LLMs have learned from vast amounts of data, which gives them the ability to generate intelligent responses on topics they have never encountered before.

In India, where multiple languages, dialects, and writing styles exist, LLMs are particularly powerful because they can understand and respond in multiple languages—be it Hindi, Tamil, Telugu, or English. This opens up endless possibilities for people across the country, from rural farmers to city-based professionals, to interact with technology in their own language.

From Traditional NLP to LLMs: The Evolution

Now, let's take a quick look at how we got to where we are today. To better understand LLMs, let's break down the journey from the early days of **Natural Language Processing (NLP)** to the development of LLMs.

1. **Traditional NLP (Before LLMs)**
   In the early stages of AI, computers could process text, but their understanding of language was very limited. Early NLP models were rule-based, meaning they relied on pre-set instructions and fixed rules to understand words. For example, if you typed in a question like, "Where is the best biryani in Hyderabad?" the system might struggle to understand and could only give you a generic response like "Hyderabad has many restaurants." The lack of context and flexibility was a major challenge.

2. **Statistical NLP (Learning from Data)**
   As technology progressed, statistical models came into play. These

models started using data (such as books, articles, and websites) to understand how words and phrases are commonly used together. For instance, these systems learned that "Hyderabad" and "biryani" often appear together, which helped them generate better responses. But still, they could not truly understand the context of a conversation or provide deep insights.

3. **Enter LLMs: Transforming Language Understanding**
   The real breakthrough came with the **transformer models**—a key innovation in the world of AI. These models could understand relationships between words across entire sentences, paragraphs, and even documents. Unlike earlier systems, which only looked at small bits of data at a time, transformers could process larger chunks of text and maintain context throughout. This led to the creation of powerful LLMs like **GPT-3** (the engine behind many modern chatbots) and **BERT** (used by Google to improve search results).

Transformers and their ability to process massive amounts of data in parallel allowed LLMs to understand language in a much deeper way, making them more flexible and effective than ever before.

Key Features That Make LLMs Stand Out

So, what makes LLMs different from other AI systems? Let's break down their most important features:

1. **Context Awareness**
   One of the key strengths of LLMs is their ability to understand **context**. If you ask a question like, "Who is the Prime Minister of India?" and then follow up with, "Where was he born?" an LLM will understand you're referring to the same person and will answer accordingly. Traditional AI models would struggle to make this connection.

2. **Creativity and Coherence**
   LLMs aren't just answering simple questions—they can also generate coherent and creative content. Whether it's writing a blog post, drafting a formal letter, or even composing poetry, LLMs can create text that is structured, engaging, and relevant. They can also adapt their tone and style depending on the request, making them versatile across different tasks.

3. **Handling Complexity**

   LLMs can tackle complex tasks. They can help you with technical subjects like mathematics or coding, draft legal documents, translate languages, summarize articles, or even engage in detailed discussions about philosophy or science.

4. **Multilingual Capabilities**

   In a country as diverse as India, where there are numerous languages spoken across the country, LLMs can work in multiple languages. Whether it's responding in English, Hindi, Tamil, or Bengali, LLMs can help bridge language barriers and make information accessible to a wider audience.

5. **Scalability**

   LLMs can handle a variety of tasks, from answering a simple question to solving problems that require deep learning and reasoning. The more data they are trained on, the better they become at providing detailed and relevant answers across a range of topics.

Why Do LLMs Matter for the Future?

LLMs are not just a technological advancement—they're a tool for empowering people. In India, where millions of people are still not familiar with English, LLMs can serve as a bridge, translating complex ideas into simpler language, allowing more people to access knowledge.

Imagine a teacher in a small town in Rajasthan using an LLM to explain complex science concepts in Hindi. Or an entrepreneur in Kochi using an LLM to generate content for their new business website. LLMs are not just making life easier for those in big cities; they are empowering people from all walks of life to interact with AI and make better decisions.

XII
The Science Behind LLMs

Understanding Transformers: The Foundation of LLMs

Imagine you're having a conversation with a friend. You talk, and they listen, picking up not just the words you say, but also understanding the context—what you're really asking, the tone of your voice, and the hidden meaning behind your words. In the world of AI, we call this **contextual understanding**, and it's one of the most important things that sets Large Language Models (LLMs) apart from earlier forms of AI.

At the heart of this remarkable ability is something called the **transformer** model. You might wonder, "What's a transformer?" No, it's not the robot cars from your favorite movie, but it's just as cool!

In simple terms, transformers are a type of AI architecture designed to understand and generate language with remarkable accuracy. Before transformers, AI struggled to maintain context in long sentences or multiple paragraphs. They'd forget what you said at the start of the conversation by the time you reached the middle. This is where transformers made a game-changing difference.

Transformers allow LLMs to read, remember, and interpret language not just from a sentence-by-sentence basis, but by looking at the entire context at once. Think of it like having a friend who can remember the entire story you're telling from beginning to end without getting lost or distracted. By using a powerful technique called **self-attention**, transformers focus on important words and parts of a sentence to understand meaning. This makes them much more efficient at handling complex conversations, as they can process relationships between words across long spans of text.

Tokenization, Embeddings, and Attention Mechanisms

Now, let's break down a few important steps that transformers use to process language—steps that are key to how LLMs work.

1. **Tokenization**
   Imagine reading a sentence like, "I love biryani from Hyderabad." A computer doesn't understand words the way we do. It breaks the sentence down into smaller pieces called **tokens**. These tokens can be as small as a single character or as large as a word. In our example, the sentence might be broken down into tokens like "I", "love", "biryani", "from", and "Hyderabad". This process of breaking down text into manageable pieces is called **tokenization**, and it's the first step for the AI to understand language.

2. **Embeddings**
   Once the sentence is broken into tokens, each token is transformed into a number or a set of numbers through something called **embeddings**. Think of it like turning each word into a unique fingerprint. These embeddings represent the meaning of words by encoding their relationships to other words. For instance, "biryani" might have a fingerprint that shows it's related to other food-related words, like "rice" or "spices." These embeddings help the AI understand not just individual words, but also how they relate to one another in different contexts.

3. **Attention Mechanisms**
   The magic behind transformers lies in a process called **attention mechanisms**. Imagine reading a book where some parts are more important than others, like a thrilling chapter that reveals a big twist in the story. Attention helps the AI focus on the "important" parts of a sentence or paragraph. When the model reads a sentence, it decides which words or tokens are most important for understanding the overall meaning. For example, in the sentence "I love biryani from Hyderabad," the word "biryani" might be more important than the word "from" when it comes to understanding the main idea. Attention allows the model to

zoom in on these key parts and provide a more accurate response.

Overview of Training Processes: Pre-Training, Fine-Tuning, and Reinforcement Learning

LLMs don't just magically know everything. They go through a **training process**, where they learn from a huge amount of data to understand how language works. Let's explore this process in more detail:

1. **Pre-Training**
    Think of **pre-training** as the initial schooling phase for an LLM. During this phase, the AI is fed vast amounts of text data—books, websites, articles, you name it. This is like how humans learn from reading and experiencing the world around them. The AI doesn't learn specific facts, but instead, it starts to recognize patterns, grammar, sentence structure, and the relationships between words. During pre-training, the model learns to predict the next word in a sentence. For example, if the model sees the phrase "I'm going to the market to buy some __," it learns to predict that "vegetables" or "fruits" could be the next word.

    This phase is essential for building the foundation of the model's language understanding. The more data it gets, the better it becomes at understanding the world and language in a general sense.

1. **Fine-Tuning**
    After pre-training, the model is not perfect. It's like an apprentice who needs specific guidance. This is where **fine-tuning** comes in. Fine-tuning is a process where the AI is trained on more specific data, often for particular tasks or industries. For instance, if you wanted to use an LLM for healthcare-related tasks, you would fine-tune it with medical documents and research papers. This helps the model become more specialized and give more accurate responses for that specific field.

    In India, fine-tuning could make an LLM more knowledgeable about local languages, cultural references, and context, allowing it to interact better with users in, say, a Marathi or Kannada dialect.

3. **Reinforcement Learning**

   Once the model is fine-tuned, there's another step called **reinforcement learning**. Imagine playing a video game where you get points for doing something correctly and lose points for mistakes. Reinforcement learning works in a similar way: the AI gets feedback (rewards or penalties) based on how well it does at completing tasks. Over time, it learns from its mistakes and improves its performance. In AI, this might look like a chatbot learning to provide better customer service by being rewarded for giving accurate and helpful answers. The more it learns from this feedback, the better it gets at understanding and responding in real-world situations.

Putting It All Together: How Does This Help in Real Life?

You might be wondering, "Why does all this matter? How does this science actually help me?" Well, these sophisticated processes of tokenization, embeddings, and attention mechanisms allow LLMs to do things like:

- **Answering Questions**: When you ask, "What's the weather in Hyderabad today?" the model can give you an accurate, real-time response by understanding your question, accessing relevant information, and crafting a clear answer.
- **Generating Creative Content**: Whether it's writing a poem in Hindi or crafting a business email in English, LLMs can produce natural, coherent content tailored to the task at hand.
- **Customer Support**: Imagine an AI-powered chatbot that helps answer your queries about an online shopping website. It can quickly access a database, understand your query, and provide solutions.

In short, LLMs are transforming the way we interact with machines, and the science behind them ensures that their responses are more human-like and useful.

XIII

Popular Large Language Models

Welcome to Chapter 3! In this chapter, we'll dive into some of the most well-known **Large Language Models** (LLMs) in the world today. These models are like the superheroes of the AI world—each with its unique abilities and strengths. By the end of this chapter, you'll understand the differences between them, the features that make them stand out, and the real-world ways in which they're used. Don't worry if you're not a techie; I'll explain everything in simple terms.

Let's meet our superheroes: **GPT**, **BERT**, **T5**, and a few others that are making waves.

1. GPT (Generative Pre-trained Transformer)

Let's start with **GPT**, one of the most famous and widely-used models. GPT is like the friendly, talkative assistant you see in movies or advertisements, always ready to answer your questions and help you out. The beauty of GPT lies in its ability to **generate human-like text** from a given prompt. Imagine you give GPT a few words like "Write a story about a mysterious cat." It will take those words and instantly generate a detailed, creative story for you. Cool, right?

Unique Features of GPT:

- **Generative Ability**: GPT is excellent at creating text, from writing essays to generating code. It can even finish your sentences, write poems, or suggest creative ideas.

- **Text Prediction**: It works by predicting what comes next in a sequence of words, making it incredibly good at completing incomplete thoughts.

Real-World Applications of GPT:

- **Customer Support**: Companies like banks and e-commerce websites use GPT to power their chatbots, helping customers with inquiries.
- **Content Creation**: GPT is often used in blogging, social media posts, and even to help authors with writing inspiration.
- **Education**: Students use GPT to help generate essays or practice languages. It's like having a tutor available 24/7!

2. BERT (Bidirectional Encoder Representations from Transformers)

Next up, we have **BERT**, and it's a bit different from GPT. While GPT is great at generating text, **BERT** is a model designed to **understand** the meaning of text. Think of BERT as a detective who is constantly trying to figure out the "why" and "how" behind words in a sentence.

Unique Features of BERT:

- **Contextual Understanding**: Unlike GPT, which processes text left to right (like reading a book from start to end), BERT reads text **both ways**, from left to right **and** right to left. This makes BERT exceptionally good at understanding the full context of words.
- **Question Answering**: BERT is highly effective at understanding and answering questions based on a given context. It doesn't just regurgitate information—it **understands** it.

Real-World Applications of BERT:

- **Search Engines**: Google uses BERT to improve the accuracy of search results. When you type something into Google, BERT helps the engine understand exactly what you mean, even if you phrase it in a more natural way.
- **Customer Support**: In addition to GPT, BERT is also used in chatbots to understand customer queries more deeply and provide more relevant answers.
- **Healthcare**: BERT has been used in medical applications to process and understand complex medical documents, helping doctors and

researchers find relevant information quickly.

3. T5 (Text-to-Text Transfer Transformer)

Now, let's talk about **T5**, a very versatile LLM that can do a wide variety of tasks. Think of T5 like an all-in-one tool that can handle everything from translating languages to answering questions or summarizing long paragraphs. T5 treats every task as a **text-to-text** problem. So, whether you want it to translate a sentence from English to Hindi, summarize a document, or generate an article, it treats all these tasks in the same way.

Unique Features of T5:

- **Text-to-Text Approach**: Every task, whether it's translation, summarization, or answering a question, is converted into a text transformation problem. For example, if you ask it to summarize a news article, it converts that into a task where the input is the article, and the output is a concise summary.
- **Flexibility**: Since it can handle multiple types of tasks, T5 is very flexible and adaptable.

Real-World Applications of T5:

- **Translation**: T5 can translate between multiple languages, making it valuable for global businesses or travel services.
- **Content Summarization**: It's used to quickly summarize long reports, news articles, or research papers, helping people digest large amounts of information faster.
- **Chatbots**: Some customer service bots use T5 to answer questions and provide solutions efficiently.

4. Other Notable Models

While GPT, BERT, and T5 are some of the most well-known LLMs, there are many others that serve unique purposes. Let's briefly mention a few of them:

- **XLNet**: An extension of BERT, XLNet improves on BERT's capabilities by looking at different permutations of words in a sentence. This allows XLNet to learn richer relationships between words and phrases, making it even more powerful for tasks like text classification and prediction.

- **RoBERTa**: A variant of BERT, RoBERTa tweaks BERT's training method to make it even better at understanding language. It's often used in applications that require deep text comprehension, such as sentiment analysis.
- **OpenAI Codex**: This model is fine-tuned specifically for **programming** tasks. It helps developers by suggesting code snippets, writing entire functions, and solving programming problems.

Comparing the Models: Which One Should You Choose?

Now that we've explored these popular models, you might be wondering, "Which one should I use?" Well, it really depends on what you need.

1. **Choose GPT** if you need something that can generate creative text or assist with content creation (e.g., writing articles, creating social media posts, or answering open-ended questions).
2. **Choose BERT** if your focus is on understanding language and context, especially for tasks like question answering, text classification, or improving search engine results.
3. **Choose T5** if you need a flexible tool that can handle a wide range of tasks, from translation to summarization and beyond.
4. **Choose XLNet or RoBERTa** if you need even deeper understanding and more complex language tasks, especially in industries like healthcare, finance, or research.
5. **Choose OpenAI Codex** if you're a developer and want an AI assistant that can help you write code and solve programming challenges.

Real-World Impact: How These Models Are Changing the Game

These models are not just for tech experts or AI researchers—they're making a real difference in everyday life.

- **Education**: Models like GPT and T5 are helping students with assignments, providing explanations, and even generating creative essays on various topics.

- **Healthcare**: BERT is helping doctors access relevant medical research, while models like T5 are summarizing patient records and notes, saving time for busy healthcare professionals.
- **Business**: These models are helping companies streamline operations, from automating customer support to generating personalized content for marketing.

In India, where there's a rich diversity of languages and cultures, LLMs are making a huge impact. From customer support chatbots in Hindi to educational assistants that teach students in local languages like Telugu, these models are making technology accessible to all.

In this chapter, we've met some of the most popular and powerful Large Language Models in the world. Each has its strengths and unique abilities, making them suitable for a wide range of applications. Whether you're looking for a content generator, a question-answering assistant, or a tool for deep language understanding, these models are transforming the way we interact with technology.

XIV
How LLMs Understand and Generate Language

Welcome to Chapter 4! By now, you've learned what **Large Language Models (LLMs)** are, and you've probably started to wonder: **How do these models actually understand and generate language?** In this chapter, we're going to peel back the curtain and take a closer look at the inner workings of LLMs. Don't worry, we'll break everything down in a way that's easy to understand.

Think of LLMs as sophisticated **language experts**—they know how to talk, respond, and even write in a way that feels natural. But there's a lot more going on behind the scenes. LLMs process **language in a very unique way** that allows them to generate coherent, context-aware sentences. Let's walk through the process, step by step.

1. Understanding Context: The Foundation of Language

One of the most remarkable things about LLMs is how they understand **context**. When you ask a question or provide a prompt, LLMs don't just focus on the immediate words you've used—they look at the **entire context** to give you a meaningful response. Imagine this as having a conversation with a person who remembers everything you've said so far and can keep track of the flow of the conversation.

Let's say you type: "How does the weather affect plants?" The model will not only understand the individual words (weather, affect, plants) but also consider the context of the conversation. So, if earlier you were discussing environmental science, it will know to respond with a scientific explanation rather than something unrelated like gardening tips.

How does this work?

LLMs achieve this by breaking down the sentence into smaller chunks called **tokens.** Tokens are just pieces of words or full words that are easier for the model to process. Once the model receives a prompt, it uses these tokens and the **context** from previous sentences to understand what you're asking. In short, LLMs are great at paying attention to **what comes before and after** the words, allowing them to generate **relevant responses.**

2. Sentence Structure: How LLMs Build Meaning

Now, let's talk about sentence structure. When you're speaking or writing, you follow a set of grammatical rules. You might not think about it much, but these rules help others understand you. In the same way, LLMs rely on their training to understand how words are put together to form meaningful sentences.

Imagine writing a sentence: "The cat sat on the mat." This sentence follows a basic structure: **subject (cat) + verb (sat) + object (mat).** LLMs have been trained on vast amounts of text, so they've learned the **patterns of language**—how words relate to each other, what order they should appear in, and how the meaning changes when you rearrange them.

The Role of Tokens in Sentence Structure

Tokens play a big role here. They allow the model to understand the individual meaning of words and also how they fit together to form coherent sentences. For example:

- The token for "sat" helps the model recognize that the action involves sitting.
- The token for "mat" helps the model understand the object involved in the action.

By predicting the next token in a sequence, LLMs can generate text that makes sense grammatically and contextually.

3. Token Prediction: How LLMs Generate Responses

At the heart of how LLMs generate text is **token prediction.** Here's where the magic happens: when you give an LLM a prompt, it predicts the most likely next token (word or part of a word) based on everything it has learned during training. This is a process that's repeated over and over again until a complete response is generated.

Let's walk through a simple example. If you type in the prompt: "Once upon a time, in a distant land, there was a..." The model predicts the next word based on the context of the prompt. It may predict "king" or "forest" or "village"—each prediction is based on patterns in the data the model was trained on. As the model continues predicting the next tokens, it eventually generates a full sentence or paragraph that flows logically from the prompt.

How Does It Know What to Say Next?

LLMs don't really "understand" words the way we do. Instead, they **predict** what should come next based on patterns they've learned. This is why LLMs are so fast—they don't have to process the meaning of the entire sentence before responding. They generate responses **in real-time**, predicting one token at a time. This allows them to quickly generate detailed, relevant responses.

4. Challenges Faced by LLMs: Biases, Hallucinations, and Interpretability

While LLMs are incredibly powerful, they do face some challenges. These issues arise because LLMs don't have true understanding—they just generate text based on patterns learned from data. Let's take a look at some of these challenges:

A. Biases in LLMs

Since LLMs are trained on vast amounts of text data from the internet, they can inadvertently **pick up biases** from that data. These biases can be based on gender, race, culture, and more. For example, if a model is trained on data that predominantly represents one group of people or a particular viewpoint, it might generate responses that are biased towards that perspective. This is a big concern in fields like hiring, law, or healthcare, where fairness is crucial.

Example:

If you ask an LLM about a job role, it may incorrectly generate a response that associates certain professions with specific genders (e.g., assuming women should be nurses and men should be engineers). This is an example of bias in AI, and it's something researchers are actively working to address.

B. Hallucinations: When LLMs Make Things Up

Sometimes, LLMs can generate information that **sounds plausible** but is actually **false**. This is known as "hallucination." Since LLMs predict the next word based on patterns, they can sometimes create answers that are **inaccurate or nonsensical** but sound convincing.

Example:

If you ask an LLM to summarize a historical event, it might confidently provide details that seem accurate at first glance but are completely wrong. It might make up facts or mix up dates, especially when the model doesn't have access to real-time data or verified sources.

C. Interpretability: Understanding How LLMs Make Decisions

Another challenge is **interpretability**—understanding how and why an LLM made a specific decision or generated a particular response. These models are incredibly complex, and because they process so many tokens at once, it can be difficult to explain **exactly why** they said something. This is important in industries like healthcare or finance, where understanding the reasoning behind a decision is crucial.

5. How We're Addressing These Challenges

Researchers and engineers are actively working to improve LLMs by:

- **Mitigating Bias**: They're developing techniques to identify and reduce bias in training data and responses.
- **Reducing Hallucinations**: Better training and more robust datasets are helping reduce the frequency of inaccurate responses.
- **Improving Interpretability**: There are ongoing efforts to make AI models more transparent so we can understand their decision-making processes.

While these challenges exist, LLMs are still powerful tools that can offer huge benefits in many fields. The key is to use them responsibly and with awareness of their limitations.

The Journey from Understanding to Creation

In this chapter, we've learned how LLMs understand and generate language, from predicting the next token to understanding context and sentence structure. We've also discussed some of the challenges these models face, such as biases, hallucinations, and interpretability issues. Despite these challenges, LLMs continue to revolutionize how we interact with technology, offering innovative solutions in education, business, and beyond.

XV
Applications of LLMs

Welcome to Chapter 5! Now that you have a solid understanding of **what Large Language Models (LLMs)** are and how they work, let's dive into how these models are being used in the real world. You'll see that LLMs aren't just a cool piece of technology—they're already being used to solve everyday problems, enhance productivity, and even change entire industries.

In this chapter, we'll walk through some **exciting real-world applications** of LLMs, from content creation to healthcare, and explore how businesses are using them to stay ahead of the competition. By the end of this chapter, you'll have a clear idea of just how powerful LLMs can be.

1. LLMs in Content Creation: A Writer's Best Friend

Content creation is a huge part of many industries—whether it's writing blogs, social media posts, or even books. But let's be honest: writing can sometimes be **time-consuming and tiring**, especially when you need to produce a lot of content regularly. This is where LLMs come in.

How LLMs Help in Content Creation

LLMs are experts at generating text. Given a prompt, they can produce articles, blogs, stories, and even poems. For example, if you need a blog post about the **impact of AI on education**, you can give the model a few keywords or a short prompt, and it will generate a **well-structured article** with relevant information. What's more, the generated content is often **polished** and coherent, saving content creators a lot of time.

LLMs can also help with **idea generation**. If you're stuck on what to write next, simply asking the model for suggestions can lead to fresh ideas or new angles on a topic.

Real-World Examples in Content Creation:

- **Marketing and Advertising**: Companies use LLMs to **generate catchy headlines**, **advertisement copy**, or even **personalized email campaigns** that speak directly to their customers.
- **Media Outlets**: News organizations use LLMs to **generate reports** on breaking news events quickly. These models can produce drafts that journalists can then refine, saving them valuable time.
- **Social Media Influencers**: Social media influencers often rely on LLMs to **generate captions**, **write product reviews**, and **engage with their audience**—all in a fraction of the time it would take to do manually.

2. LLMs in Customer Service: The Virtual Assistant Revolution

Anyone who's interacted with a **chatbot** or used a virtual assistant like Siri or Alexa has already experienced the magic of LLMs. These models are behind the scenes, helping businesses provide **faster and more efficient customer support**.

How LLMs Improve Customer Service

In customer service, **LLMs can process customer queries**, understand them, and provide **accurate responses**. They can help customers with everything from troubleshooting technical issues to **answering frequently asked questions (FAQs)**. Instead of waiting on hold for a human representative, customers can now get instant support from an AI-powered system.

Additionally, LLMs are great at **personalizing responses**. For example, if a customer reaches out to a company about an order, the LLM can pull up the order details and give a personalized response, making it feel as though the customer is speaking with a human representative.

Real-World Examples in Customer Service:

- **E-commerce**: Online retailers like **Amazon** use LLMs to **handle product inquiries** and **process orders**, allowing customers to get fast, 24/7 support.

- **Telecommunications**: Mobile service providers use LLMs to troubleshoot technical problems, **activate services**, or **change plans** without needing a human agent.
- **Banking**: Banks use LLMs for **chatbots** that can help customers with things like checking account balances, paying bills, or even **answering questions about loans**.

3. LLMs in Education: Personalizing Learning

Education is an area where LLMs can have a **huge impact**. Traditional education systems often use a one-size-fits-all approach, but with LLMs, learning can be **personalized**, engaging, and more effective for each student.

How LLMs Transform Education

LLMs can **assist in tutoring** by answering students' questions, explaining concepts in simpler terms, or offering **additional learning materials**. Imagine a student struggling with math. Instead of simply reading a textbook, they can interact with an AI model that explains complex concepts in a way that's easier to understand. This can make learning feel more **interactive** and **tailored** to individual needs.

LLMs are also used to create **intelligent study assistants** that help students **prepare for exams** or **practice a new language**. The model can provide **instant feedback** on practice exercises, explain why an answer is correct or incorrect, and even offer suggestions for improvement.

Real-World Examples in Education:

- **Online Learning Platforms**: Platforms like **Khan Academy** or **Coursera** use LLMs to provide students with **interactive quizzes** or to generate personalized **study plans** based on their performance.
- **Language Learning Apps**: Apps like **Duolingo** use LLMs to create personalized language lessons, practice exercises, and interactive conversations.
- **Homework Help**: Students can use AI-powered apps to **get real-time answers** to homework questions, complete with explanations.

4. LLMs in Healthcare: Revolutionizing Patient Care

In the healthcare industry, LLMs are making **huge strides** in improving patient care, diagnosing diseases, and even assisting in medical research.

How LLMs Aid Healthcare

LLMs are used to **analyze medical records**, **identify patterns in patient data**, and even **predict potential health issues**. For example, by analyzing a patient's medical history, LLMs can **suggest possible diagnoses** or recommend **treatment plans** based on current medical knowledge. This can assist doctors in making faster, more accurate decisions.

LLMs are also used in **telemedicine** for virtual consultations. Patients can interact with an AI-powered system to describe their symptoms and get initial advice before they even see a doctor.

Real-World Examples in Healthcare:

- **Medical Research**: LLMs are helping researchers **analyze large datasets** of clinical trials and **discover new treatments** or **identify drug interactions**.
- **Diagnostic Assistance**: AI-powered systems like **IBM Watson Health** help doctors analyze patient data and suggest possible diagnoses, speeding up the decision-making process.
- **Virtual Healthcare**: Telemedicine platforms are using LLMs to **triage patients**, offer **symptom checkers**, and even **schedule appointments**.

5. LLMs in Legal Services: Streamlining Legal Processes

In the legal world, LLMs are changing the way lawyers work. With their ability to process large amounts of text, LLMs can help **research case laws**, **draft legal documents**, and even **assist in contract analysis**.

How LLMs Support Legal Services

Lawyers traditionally spend hours reading case files and legal documents to find relevant information. With LLMs, these tasks can be automated. LLMs can **analyze thousands of legal documents** in seconds and extract relevant information for a case. They can even generate legal briefs, **summarize**

contracts, and assist in **drafting legal opinions**.

Real-World Examples in Legal Services:

- **Contract Review**: Legal firms use LLMs to **automatically review contracts** for specific terms, risks, or inconsistencies, saving time and improving accuracy.
- **Legal Research**: LLMs can **search vast databases** of legal cases and help lawyers find precedents or case laws relevant to a client's situation.
- **Compliance Monitoring**: LLMs can help businesses stay compliant with regulations by analyzing **legal documents** and flagging any changes or potential legal issues.

6. LLMs in Financial Services: Enhancing Decision-Making

The financial industry is another area where LLMs are making a big impact. These models can assist with everything from **predicting market trends** to **analyzing financial reports** and even **automating customer support**.

How LLMs Help in Finance

In finance, LLMs help by analyzing large volumes of data quickly, making predictions about stock prices, and even offering personalized investment advice. They can also assist with **risk assessment**, helping financial institutions evaluate potential risks in loans, investments, or other financial activities.

Real-World Examples in Financial Services:

- **Algorithmic Trading**: Investment firms use LLMs to **analyze market trends** and make **real-time trading decisions** based on large datasets.
- **Credit Risk Assessment**: Banks use LLMs to assess the **creditworthiness** of loan applicants by analyzing their financial history and generating risk profiles.
- **Financial Advising**: LLMs can provide customers with **personalized financial advice**, whether it's about saving, investing, or retirement

planning.

The Versatility of LLMs

In this chapter, we've explored the wide range of **real-world applications** of Large Language Models. From content creation to healthcare and beyond, LLMs are making a significant impact across many industries, helping businesses operate more efficiently, making services more accessible, and improving decision-making processes.

As we continue to see more innovations in LLM technology, expect to see even **greater integration** in areas like **law**, **education**, and **healthcare**, enhancing the way we live, work

XVI
Ethical Considerations in LLMs

Welcome to Chapter 6! Now that we've explored the incredible power and potential of **Large Language Models (LLMs)**, it's time to tackle an equally important topic: **ethics.** With great power comes great responsibility, and as LLMs continue to shape various industries, it's crucial to address the ethical challenges that arise.

In this chapter, we'll take a deep dive into some of the most pressing ethical concerns surrounding LLMs, including **bias**, **privacy**, and **responsible usage**. By the end of this chapter, you'll not only understand the challenges we face with AI, but also why it's vital to approach the development and deployment of these models with care.

1. Bias in LLMs: The Risk of Unfairness

Imagine if you walked into a store and found that every product was designed specifically for one type of person—perhaps a certain gender, race, or age group. How would you feel? This is the kind of bias we're concerned about when we talk about AI models.

What is Bias in LLMs?

LLMs, like all AI models, learn by **analyzing vast amounts of data**. They don't inherently "know" what's right or wrong—they learn patterns based on the data they are trained on. However, the data used to train these models may carry **historical biases**. For example, if an LLM is trained on text that has been written by humans, it might learn biased viewpoints, stereotypes, or unfair associations. These biases can be about anything—gender, race, religion, or even socio-economic status.

Let's take an example: imagine using an LLM to generate a job advertisement. If the training data contains subtle biases where job descriptions for leadership roles are often associated with certain genders or ethnic backgrounds, the AI might unintentionally suggest a description that excludes others. This could result in **discrimination**, even though the AI itself is just following patterns it's learned from the data.

Why is this a Problem?

When AI systems reflect and amplify biases, it can perpetuate **unfair treatment** of people from certain groups. This can lead to **discriminatory practices** in recruitment, healthcare, finance, and even in everyday applications like customer service. Bias in AI can harm individuals and **reinforce existing inequalities** in society.

2. Privacy Concerns and Data Security: Protecting Personal Information

With LLMs processing large volumes of text data, there's an inherent risk of **exposing sensitive information**. In the process of learning from text, AI models might inadvertently "leak" personal or private details that shouldn't be accessible to everyone.

What Are the Privacy Concerns?

LLMs are trained on massive datasets, which could include everything from books and articles to social media posts and private conversations. If sensitive personal data, such as names, addresses, or health information, is included in the training data, there's a possibility that the AI model could inadvertently generate content that includes private details. For instance, if someone asks the model for information about a specific event or person, the AI might generate **inappropriate or unintended responses** that violate privacy.

Moreover, when people interact with LLMs, they might share personal data, like questions about health, finances, or personal preferences. If the data is not handled properly, it could **compromise users' privacy**.

How Do We Protect Privacy?

To protect privacy, it's essential that LLMs are **trained** using **anonymized data**—data that is stripped of personal identifiers. Additionally, strong **data security protocols** need to be in place to ensure that any data collected through user interactions is kept safe and used responsibly. Users should also have clear control over what data is shared with AI systems, and AI developers must prioritize **user consent** and **transparency**.

3. Responsible Use and Regulation of LLMs: Setting Boundaries

As LLMs become more powerful, it's vital to ensure they are being used responsibly. **Responsible AI usage** means ensuring that LLMs are not used to spread **misinformation**, **manipulate opinions**, or cause harm in any way.

The Need for Regulation

Right now, there are no **global laws** or consistent regulations on the use of LLMs. As AI continues to evolve, it's crucial that governments, companies, and organizations come together to create **guidelines** and **ethical standards** for their use. This includes putting in place policies to prevent malicious uses of AI, such as:

- **Deepfake creation**: AI models could be used to generate false or misleading media, creating deepfakes that manipulate people's perceptions or opinions.
- **Misinformation**: LLMs could potentially be used to spread false news or fake information on social media or websites.

The challenge lies in creating **ethical regulations** that don't stifle innovation but ensure that AI is used for good. AI regulations should aim to:

- Promote **fairness** and **accountability**.
- Prevent AI from being used in harmful ways.
- Ensure transparency and **explainability** of AI systems, so we can understand how they make decisions.

How Do We Use LLMs Responsibly?

For businesses and developers working with LLMs, it's important to ensure that AI models are used in ways that **align with ethical standards**. This means:

- **Auditing AI systems** for biases regularly.
- **Testing** the models to ensure they aren't inadvertently causing harm.
- **Educating** users on how to use AI ethically and responsibly.

Businesses should also be transparent about **how data is collected** and **how AI is being used**, ensuring that users are fully informed.

4. How Can We Ensure Ethical LLM Development?

The development of LLMs is a **collective responsibility**. Developers, companies, governments, and individuals must work together to ensure that AI benefits everyone while minimizing risks.

Ethical AI Development Best Practices

To promote responsible AI development, consider the following practices:

- **Bias Audits**: Regularly audit the AI model to identify and remove biases from the training data.
- **Diverse Data**: Train LLMs on diverse datasets that represent a broad range of cultures, languages, and viewpoints, ensuring fairness.
- **Human-in-the-loop (HITL)**: In some critical applications (like healthcare or legal), have humans involved in the decision-making process to catch any errors or biases the AI might introduce.
- **Transparency**: Developers should be clear about the capabilities and limitations of their models, as well as how data is being collected and used.

Collaboration Across Sectors

Governments, businesses, and the **AI research community** need to collaborate to establish ethical guidelines, share best practices, and promote responsible AI innovation. International cooperation is necessary to create **global frameworks** for ethical AI, especially since AI has far-reaching implications across borders.

Building a Responsible Future with LLMs

As we've seen, LLMs have the potential to revolutionize many areas of our lives, from healthcare to education to customer service. But as with all technologies, we must be vigilant and mindful of the ethical challenges they present.

By addressing issues like **bias**, **privacy**, and **responsible use**, we can ensure that LLMs are developed and deployed in ways that are beneficial, equitable, and ethical. **Responsible AI** is not just about creating advanced technologies, but also about creating a future where **everyone** can benefit from AI without fear of harm or unfair treatment.

XVII
Challenges in Scaling LLMs

Welcome to Chapter 7! By now, you've learned about the incredible capabilities of **Large Language Models (LLMs)**—how they understand and generate human-like text. But as these models grow more advanced and widespread, scaling them comes with its own set of **challenges**. In this chapter, we'll discuss the main hurdles faced when scaling LLMs, including **computational costs**, **data sourcing**, and **integration complexities**. Don't worry—we'll break it all down in a way that's easy to understand, even if you don't have a technical background.

Let's get started!

1. The High Computational and Environmental Costs of Training LLMs

Imagine you're baking a cake. The more ingredients you add, the more time it takes, and the bigger the oven you'll need. Training an LLM is very similar—except instead of an oven, you're using huge amounts of **computational power**, and the ingredients are **data**.

Why Is Training an LLM So Expensive?

Training LLMs requires enormous amounts of data and time. In fact, it's a **resource-intensive process**. To give you an idea of what's involved, consider the following:

- **Massive computational resources**: To train a large-scale language model like GPT-3, you need powerful computer systems equipped with thousands of **Graphics Processing Units (GPUs)** or **Tensor Processing Units (TPUs)**. These are specialized hardware components designed to perform calculations quickly. The cost of renting or owning such high-end equipment is **extremely high**.
- **Electricity and cooling**: Just like how a high-performance gaming PC consumes a lot of electricity, the servers running these large models need a constant supply of power. This also generates heat, meaning **cooling systems** are required to prevent overheating, adding further to the cost.
- **Environmental impact**: The energy consumption involved in training LLMs raises concerns about their environmental footprint. The more power these models consume, the higher their **carbon emissions**. In a world that's increasingly focused on sustainability, these environmental costs are something developers are taking seriously.

The Cost in Numbers

To put things into perspective, **training GPT-3**, one of the most well-known LLMs, is estimated to cost millions of dollars. This doesn't include the **operational costs** of running the model after it's trained, which are also substantial.

As a result, only large tech companies and well-funded organizations can afford to build and maintain these powerful models. But, these high costs also mean that scaling LLMs for wider use requires finding **more efficient ways** to reduce these expenses.

2. Data Sourcing and Annotation Complexities

Training LLMs requires **a lot of data**—and not just any data, but **high-quality, diverse, and representative data**. Think of it like this: if you're teaching a child about the world, you wouldn't just show them a few examples. You'd expose them to a wide variety of experiences and viewpoints.

Data Sourcing: Where Does the Data Come From?

The first challenge in scaling LLMs is **data sourcing**. To train a model like GPT-3, developers need access to **huge datasets** containing text from books, articles, websites, and more. But sourcing data isn't as simple as just grabbing a bunch of random texts. The data needs to be:

- **Diverse**: LLMs should be exposed to a broad range of topics, languages, cultures, and ideas to ensure they can generate relevant responses to any query.
- **Accurate**: The data must be factual and high-quality. If the data is flawed or biased, the model will generate flawed or biased responses.
- **Representative**: Data should reflect the real-world diversity of thoughts and experiences, so the model doesn't learn harmful stereotypes or biases.

Data Annotation: Making Sense of the Data

Once the data is collected, it often needs to be **annotated**. Annotation is the process of tagging data with labels or categories that make it easier for the model to understand. For example, if the model is learning to recognize questions in a conversation, human annotators might label certain sentences as "questions" and others as "statements."

This process can be **time-consuming and expensive**. It also requires **expert annotators** who understand the nuances of language, culture, and context. For large models, the annotation process can involve tens of thousands of hours of work, making it a significant challenge in scaling LLMs.

3. Scalability and Integration with Other AI Systems

Now that we have a trained model, how do we scale it to serve a wide variety of applications? The answer is **integration**—but scaling LLMs so that they can work seamlessly with other AI systems or applications comes with its own set of difficulties.

How Do We Scale LLMs?

Once an LLM is trained, the next challenge is ensuring that it can be deployed and used efficiently by **millions of users**. Imagine trying to handle thousands of customers in a store at the same time. You need to make sure the systems are fast, responsive, and can manage high demand without crashing. In the world of AI, this means:

- **Infrastructure**: Ensuring that the computational infrastructure can handle the high demand for processing requests in real-time. This may require large cloud-based systems with powerful servers that can handle multiple requests simultaneously.

- **Latency**: LLMs need to provide **quick responses**. If the model is slow to generate text, it can disrupt user experience. Developers need to ensure that scaling the model doesn't come at the expense of response time.

Integrating LLMs with Other AI Systems

For many organizations, LLMs are just one part of a larger AI ecosystem. For example, a chatbot might use an LLM to generate responses but also rely on other AI systems for things like voice recognition or image processing.

Integrating these systems can be tricky. Developers need to ensure that all the systems can **communicate with each other** and share information seamlessly. This might involve developing **APIs (Application Programming Interfaces)** that allow the LLM to work alongside other tools, platforms, and databases.

Scaling LLMs for the Future

As we've discussed, scaling LLMs is no simple feat. The challenges—whether it's the **high computational costs**, the **complexities of data sourcing**, or the **integration with other AI systems**—are significant. But that doesn't mean these challenges are insurmountable. As technology continues to advance, researchers are finding ways to make LLMs more efficient, cost-effective, and accessible.

In the coming years, we can expect new innovations that will make it easier to **scale LLMs** and bring their capabilities to more people and industries. The future of LLMs is bright, and with continued focus on **reducing costs**, **improving data handling**, and **seamlessly integrating AI systems**, we can unlock even greater potential.

XVIII

The Future of LLMs

Welcome to Chapter 8, where we look ahead to the exciting future of **Large Language Models (LLMs)**. As we've seen so far, LLMs have already made a huge impact in various fields like business, healthcare, education, and entertainment. But what's next? What will the future of these models look like? How will they evolve, and what challenges and opportunities lie ahead?

In this chapter, we'll dive into the predictions about **advancements in LLM architecture**, the **road to Artificial General Intelligence (AGI)**, and the growing importance of **open-source** and **community-driven LLMs**. Don't worry—we'll keep things simple and conversational, so you can follow along without needing a tech background.

1. Predictions About Advancements in LLM Architecture

We've come a long way since the first language models were developed. But just as smartphones have evolved from simple devices to powerful computers in our pockets, LLMs too are continuously improving. So, what might the **next generation** of LLMs look like?

Improved Understanding and Context

One of the biggest advancements we can expect is the **ability to understand context more deeply**. Currently, LLMs can process a lot of information, but their comprehension of long-term context—how information relates to past statements or conversations—can still be limited.

In the future, LLMs may be able to:

- **Remember past interactions**: Just like how you might recall a conversation you had with a friend yesterday, future LLMs could remember previous conversations with users, allowing for more personalized and meaningful interactions.

- **Understand subtle nuances**: LLMs will get better at picking up on things like **tone, humor, and sarcasm**. This could make AI assistants more conversational and human-like.

Multimodal Models

Another exciting development is the growth of **multimodal models**. Right now, most LLMs focus on text, but in the future, we might see models that can handle multiple types of input—like text, images, and audio—all at once.

- **For example**: Imagine asking an AI to **analyze a photo**, describe what's happening in it, and provide recommendations based on the context of the image and text input you've given. This could revolutionize everything from customer service to content creation, where users can interact with AI in **multiple ways**.

Energy Efficiency

With LLMs requiring massive computational power, energy consumption is a growing concern. As technology advances, one of the goals will be to **make these models more energy-efficient** without sacrificing performance. **Research into more sustainable AI architecture** could lead to breakthroughs that reduce the carbon footprint of training and running these models.

2. The Road to Artificial General Intelligence (AGI)

You've probably heard the term **Artificial General Intelligence (AGI)** floating around. It's a big topic in the world of AI, and you may be wondering, what exactly is AGI, and how does it relate to LLMs?

What Is AGI?

In simple terms, **AGI** refers to an AI system that can perform any task that a human can do. While current LLMs are great at specific tasks—like generating text, answering questions, or writing code—they are still limited by the data they were trained on and the specific tasks they're designed to do.

AGI, on the other hand, would be a **truly intelligent machine** capable of understanding and reasoning about the world in the same way humans do. It would have the ability to **learn from experience**, adapt to new situations, and apply knowledge across different fields without being explicitly programmed.

Are LLMs on the Road to AGI?

LLMs, as they are now, are not quite AGI, but they are a significant **step in that direction**. They represent a form of **narrow AI**—highly specialized AI that excels at particular tasks but cannot operate outside those boundaries. However, the evolution of LLMs—particularly their ability to understand and generate more sophisticated outputs—could be part of the journey towards AGI.

That said, we're still a long way from true AGI. The road ahead will require breakthroughs in several areas, such as:

- **Self-awareness**: For AGI to work, it will need to understand itself, its actions, and its environment—something current models can't do.
- **Reasoning and abstract thinking**: AGI will need to process and make sense of complex, abstract ideas the way humans do.

Researchers in the field are optimistic, but many agree that **AGI is still a long-term goal**, one that might take decades to achieve (or maybe even longer).

3. The Role of Open-Source and Community-Driven LLMs

As LLMs continue to advance, we are likely to see a greater **shift towards open-source models**. This is an exciting development for several reasons, especially in terms of **democratizing access to AI**.

What Is Open-Source LLM?

An **open-source LLM** is one where the code and data used to train the model are freely available to anyone. This allows developers and researchers worldwide to contribute to improving the model, share insights, and use the technology for their own purposes.

For example, there are several open-source LLMs like **GPT-Neo** and **BLOOM**, which are being developed by communities rather than just large tech companies. This shift allows:

- **More diverse input**: Open-source projects allow more people from different backgrounds, cultures, and countries to participate in the development process, which can lead to **more inclusive and unbiased models.**
- **Faster innovation**: With contributions from a large, global community, open-source LLMs can evolve quickly. Researchers and developers can share breakthroughs and tools, which means new techniques and improvements spread fast.
- **Lower barriers to entry**: Open-source LLMs allow smaller organizations, startups, and even individuals to experiment with advanced AI without needing huge financial resources.

The Future of Open-Source AI

The future will likely see an even **greater emphasis on open-source** as the AI community recognizes the benefits of collaboration. This movement can help solve some of the challenges we face today, such as biases in AI, a lack of diverse perspectives in training data, and the monopolization of AI by a few large corporations.

Moreover, open-source LLMs will play an important role in fields like **education**, **research**, and **personal development**, enabling a wide range of applications without the barrier of high costs.

The Future Looks Bright

The future of **Large Language Models** is full of **exciting possibilities**. As we continue to advance in model architecture, we can expect LLMs to become more intelligent, more contextually aware, and more integrated into our daily lives. The journey towards **Artificial General Intelligence** will continue, but we're still many years away from achieving it. In the meantime, open-source LLMs will allow more people to explore, experiment, and innovate, accelerating AI advancements for the benefit of everyone.

As the technology matures, we'll see **LLMs embedded in all aspects of society**—from helping with education and healthcare to providing creative assistance and supporting businesses. The key will be to manage these advancements responsibly, ensuring that AI benefits humanity while minimizing its risks.

Core Applications of AI and Generative AI

XIX

AI in Everyday Life

"AI is not the future; AI is the present we are already living in."

If I told you that you interact with Artificial Intelligence (AI) every single day, would you believe me? Whether you're asking Siri for the weather, scrolling through your Instagram feed, or watching Netflix after dinner, AI is quietly working behind the scenes. It's no longer a futuristic concept in sci-fi movies—AI is woven into the fabric of our lives, making things faster, smarter, and more personalized.

This chapter will help you discover how AI powers the world around you, often in ways you may not even notice. Together, let's break down the invisible magic of AI in our smartphones, social media, online shopping, and even our homes.

1. AI in Your Smartphone: Your Smartest Companion

Let's start with the device in your pocket or hand—the smartphone. Have you ever wondered why your phone feels so smart?

- **Voice Assistants**:
Think of Apple's Siri, Google Assistant, or Amazon Alexa. When you say, *"Hey Google, set a timer for 10 minutes,"* AI processes your speech, understands your intent, and responds instantly. These virtual assistants are powered by **Natural Language Processing (NLP)**, allowing them to "hear," "understand," and "talk" back to you in natural language.

Even more impressive, they learn from you! If you frequently ask about cricket scores, your assistant might start anticipating these requests or prioritize cricket news in its responses.

- **Face Unlock and Biometrics**:
  Have you noticed how quickly your phone unlocks when it detects your face? That's AI-powered **facial recognition** at work. The camera captures your face, analyzes its unique features, and matches it with stored data—all in a split second.
- **Autocorrect and Predictive Text**:
  Ever wondered how your phone "knows" what you're about to type? AI algorithms predict the words you're likely to type based on your past behavior. For example, if you frequently text *"See you soon!"*, your phone might suggest it as soon as you type *"See…"*.
- **Camera Enhancements**:
  Whether it's Apple, Samsung, or Google, smartphone cameras are smarter than ever, thanks to AI. Features like portrait mode, night mode, and even real-time beauty filters use AI to improve your photos. They analyze lighting, depth, and colors to produce stunning images.

2. Search Engines: Finding What You Need, Instantly

Have you noticed how Google seems to know exactly what you're looking for—even when you type just a few words? That's AI in action.

- **Understanding Your Search**:
  Let's say you type *"best dosa in Hyderabad"*. Google doesn't just look for websites with those exact words. Its AI understands your intent and gives you restaurant suggestions, maps, reviews, and even popular dishes.
- **Personalization**:
  Search engines don't treat everyone the same. AI learns from your previous searches and browsing habits to deliver results tailored just for you. For example, if you love technology blogs, searching *"latest news"* might prioritize tech news for you.
- **Voice Search**:
  Instead of typing, many of us now say, *"Google, what's the capital of Telangana?"*. AI-powered **speech recognition** understands the question and quickly fetches the answer—Hyderabad, of course!

3. Social Media: The Invisible AI That Keeps You Scrolling

Think about how much time you spend on Instagram, Facebook, or YouTube. Have you ever wondered why you can't stop scrolling? That's AI working its magic.

- **Personalized Feeds**:
  Platforms like Facebook, Instagram, and Twitter use AI algorithms to curate your feed. They analyze your likes, shares, comments, and time spent on posts to show you content they think you'll love.

  For example, if you often like cooking videos, your Instagram Explore page might flood you with tasty recipes and food hacks.

- **Recommendation Systems**:
  YouTube and Netflix use **AI recommendation engines** to keep you hooked. Ever noticed how YouTube suggests the "perfect" next video, or how Netflix recommends shows based on what you've watched? AI analyzes your viewing habits, compares them with millions of other users, and predicts what you'll enjoy next.

- **Content Moderation**:
  AI also helps keep social media safe. It automatically detects and flags harmful or inappropriate content like hate speech or violent images.

4. AI in E-Commerce: Making Online Shopping Smarter

Ever noticed how Amazon, Flipkart, or Myntra seem to *know* what you want to buy? That's AI enhancing your online shopping experience.

- **Personalized Recommendations**:
  Have you searched for *"running shoes"* on Amazon? The next time you log in, Amazon might suggest sportswear, fitness trackers, or socks. AI analyzes your browsing behavior and purchase history to recommend products you're likely to buy.

- **Chatbots for Customer Support**:
  Many online stores use AI-powered chatbots to assist you 24/7. Whether you're asking, *"Where's my order?"* or *"Is this product available?"*, chatbots provide instant answers, saving you time.

- **Dynamic Pricing**:
  AI enables dynamic pricing, where prices of products fluctuate based

on demand, competition, or your browsing habits. For example, flight tickets might increase if demand spikes during festive seasons.

5. AI in Smart Homes and Autonomous Vehicles

AI is even changing the way we live at home and travel on the road.

- **Smart Homes**:
  Devices like **Amazon Alexa**, **Google Nest**, or smart appliances use AI to automate tasks. You can say, *"Alexa, turn on the lights,"* or schedule your AC to cool the room before you arrive home. AI also learns your patterns—if you lower the lights every evening at 7 PM, it might start doing it automatically.
- **Autonomous Vehicles**:
  Self-driving cars use AI to "see" the road, identify obstacles, and make driving decisions. Sensors, cameras, and AI algorithms work together to ensure safety. While fully autonomous cars are still being tested, features like **driver-assist**, automatic braking, and parking assistance are already powered by AI.

Bringing It All Together

Artificial Intelligence has seamlessly integrated into our daily lives, often without us realizing it. From smartphones to social media, from online shopping to smart homes, AI makes things faster, smarter, and more convenient.

The beauty of AI lies in its ability to adapt and learn. Every interaction you have with a virtual assistant, every video you watch, and every product you buy trains AI systems to serve you better.

As India rapidly adopts AI, cities like Hyderabad, Bengaluru, and Chennai are becoming innovation hubs. AI is not just for tech-savvy people—it's for everyone, from students and teachers to small business owners and homemakers.

XX
Generative AI in Creativity

"The creative adult is the child who survived, but now AI is that new child learning to create with us."

When you think of art, music, writing, or films, what comes to mind? Probably a painter in front of a canvas, a musician composing melodies on a piano, or a writer staring at a blinking cursor. For centuries, creativity has been seen as a *uniquely human* ability, the very thing that sets us apart from machines. But what if I told you that Artificial Intelligence (AI) can now write poetry, compose music, paint pictures, and even help create films?

Yes, it's happening—and it's called **Generative AI**. These intelligent systems are not here to replace artists and writers but to work *with* them, sparking ideas and pushing the boundaries of creativity in ways we never imagined.

In this chapter, we'll explore how generative AI is revolutionizing creative industries, from art and music to literature and film. Don't worry—you don't need to be an artist or techie to understand. We'll break everything down in a simple, conversational way.

1. What Is Generative AI? And Why Does It Matter?

Before we dive into AI-powered creativity, let's understand what **Generative AI** means.

Imagine you give a computer some examples of paintings, stories, or music. Instead of just analyzing those examples, the computer "learns" the style and then *generates something new* on its own—a new painting, story, or song. That's what generative AI does.

It's like teaching a robot how to cook a biryani. After watching you make it a few times, the robot starts experimenting, creating its own version of the dish. It might even surprise you with some creative twists—perhaps it adds a secret spice or serves it differently. Generative AI works similarly but with data like images, text, and sounds.

This technology uses models like **GANs (Generative Adversarial Networks)** and **Large Language Models (LLMs)** to generate content that is original yet inspired by what it has learned.

2. AI in Art: Can a Machine Be Creative?

Have you ever heard of an AI painting selling for millions of dollars? It's true! In 2018, a painting created by AI—called *"Portrait of Edmond de Belamy"*—sold for $432,500 at an auction. But how did AI paint it?

- **How It Works**:
Generative AI models like **DALL·E** or **MidJourney** learn from thousands of artworks. They analyze colors, styles, brush strokes, and patterns. When you give them a prompt like *"Paint a cat sitting under the stars in Van Gogh's style"*, they generate an entirely new artwork that resembles what you requested.
- **AI Collaborating with Artists**:
Many artists are now collaborating with AI to explore new styles and concepts. For example:

  ◦ An artist might use AI to generate ideas for sketches.
  ◦ AI tools can create digital art quickly, which the artist then refines.

"AI doesn't replace creativity—it amplifies it." Artists now have a digital assistant that inspires them and helps them explore ideas they might not have thought of alone.

Real-World Example:

- AI-powered tools like **DeepArt** and **Runway ML** allow anyone—whether you're an artist or not—to generate stunning visuals with just a few clicks.

3. AI in Music: From Beethoven to Beats

Imagine a world where AI composes symphonies, writes pop songs, or even creates background scores for movies. Sounds futuristic? It's already happening.

- **How AI Makes Music:**
Generative AI models analyze massive amounts of music data—classical compositions, pop hits, jazz solos, or EDM beats. They learn musical patterns like rhythm, harmony, and melodies. Then, they create completely original music based on those patterns.

For example:

  - AI can generate soothing piano music inspired by Beethoven.
  - It can create a catchy pop tune that sounds like your favorite singer's style.

- **AI Collaborating with Musicians:**
Musicians are now using AI as a creative partner. Imagine you're stuck on a melody. AI tools like **AIVA** or **Amper Music** can generate options for you to experiment with. AI doesn't replace the musician; it enhances their creative process.

Real-World Example:

- The song *"Daddy's Car"* was created entirely by AI in the style of The Beatles. Musicians then added human touches to refine it.

4. AI in Writing: From Poetry to Stories

Writing is another area where generative AI is making waves. From blog posts and marketing copy to poems and short stories, AI tools like **ChatGPT** are helping writers generate ideas, drafts, and even finished pieces.

- **How It Works:**
AI language models like **GPT-4** analyze billions of words—books, articles, and stories. They learn how sentences are structured and how ideas flow. When you give them a prompt like, *"Write a mystery story about a hidden treasure"*, they create an entirely new story for you.

- **AI as a Writing Assistant**:
  Writers now use AI tools to:

  - Overcome writer's block.
  - Brainstorm story ideas or character names.
  - Edit and polish drafts quickly.

"AI doesn't take away your voice—it helps you find it." AI-generated writing is like having a brainstorming buddy that never runs out of ideas.
Real-World Example:

- Newspapers like *The Guardian* use AI to write data-heavy reports.
- Authors use AI tools to co-write novels or generate creative prompts.

5. AI in Film and Video: A New Era of Creativity

AI is even stepping into filmmaking and video production, transforming how movies are made.

- **AI in Scriptwriting**:
  Tools like **Sudowrite** can help writers brainstorm dialogue or plot points for their screenplays. Imagine telling AI: *"Write a thrilling scene where a detective finds a clue"*, and it generates ideas to build on.
- **AI for Visual Effects**:
  Filmmakers use AI to enhance visual effects (VFX). AI can generate realistic backgrounds, characters, or even creatures in sci-fi and fantasy movies.
- **Deepfakes and AI in Video Creation**:
  AI tools can now create realistic videos or animations, opening new possibilities in storytelling. While deepfakes raise ethical concerns, they also show how powerful AI has become in visual arts.

Real-World Example:

- Filmmakers used AI to digitally recreate the voice of actor Anthony Bourdain in the documentary *"Roadrunner"*.

6. The Future of AI in Creativity

Generative AI is still evolving, but it's clear that it will play a huge role in the future of creativity. Here's what's exciting:

- **Accessibility**: Anyone—regardless of skill—can use AI to create art, music, or writing. AI democratizes creativity.
- **New Creative Frontiers**: AI will push humans to explore ideas and mediums we haven't even imagined yet.
- **Collaboration, Not Competition**: The future isn't AI *vs.* humans; it's AI *with* humans, creating together.

Final Thoughts

Generative AI in creativity is a beautiful blend of technology and imagination. It's not here to replace artists, musicians, or writers but to empower them with tools that amplify their creative power. Whether you're a professional creator or just someone who loves to dabble in art or music, AI is like a limitless toolbox ready for you to explore.

As we look to the future, the possibilities are endless. Imagine creating art, composing music, or writing stories with the help of AI—making creativity accessible to everyone.

So, are you ready to create something new? AI is here to help you turn your ideas into reality. Let your imagination take flight!

XXI

AI and Generative AI in Business

Imagine walking into a modern office, but instead of paper stacks and overworked employees juggling tasks, you see teams using AI-powered tools to make decisions faster, serve customers better, and even predict the future. Sounds futuristic? Not anymore.

Artificial Intelligence (AI), and more specifically **Generative AI**, has already become an invisible co-worker in many organizations. Whether you realize it or not, businesses—big and small—are leveraging AI to improve operations, generate content, analyze data, and boost customer satisfaction.

But what does this look like in practice? How does AI help businesses make better decisions or automate workflows? If you're a non-tech person, don't worry—I'm going to break this down for you with examples and a conversational tone. You're about to see how AI is not just for tech giants but for *everyone* looking to do better business.

Let's dive in!

1. AI in Business Analytics: Making Smarter Decisions

Have you ever wondered how businesses decide where to open a new store, how much stock to keep, or what price to sell their products at? The answer lies in **data**. Businesses collect tons of data, but turning all that data into insights is where AI comes in.

- **What AI Does**:
  AI systems analyze massive amounts of data in seconds—things that would take humans weeks or even months. AI can:

  - Spot trends and patterns.
  - Forecast future outcomes (predict sales or demand).
  - Suggest actions based on data.

  For example:

- A retail store uses AI to analyze customer data and identify which products sell best on weekends versus weekdays. This helps them stock shelves accordingly.
- Restaurants use AI to predict busy hours and optimize staff schedules.

Business in Action:

- Companies like Amazon use AI-powered tools to forecast inventory and predict customer demand, which is why they rarely run out of popular items.

"Data is the new oil, but AI is the engine that refines it into something valuable."

2. AI in Customer Service: The Rise of Chatbots and Virtual Assistants

How many times have you chatted with a customer support agent online and thought, *"Are you really a person?"* Chances are, you were talking to an AI chatbot.

- **What AI Does**:
  Chatbots and virtual assistants powered by **Natural Language Processing (NLP)** help businesses serve customers 24/7.

  - They answer common questions.
  - Solve basic issues (like resetting a password).
  - Redirect complex queries to human agents.

Example:

- When you message a brand on WhatsApp or chat on their website, AI chatbots respond instantly: *"How can I help you today?"* These bots handle thousands of queries simultaneously, something no human team could do alone.
- **Virtual Assistants**: AI tools like Siri, Alexa, and Google Assistant have also entered business settings. Imagine asking your assistant, *"What were last quarter's sales?"* and getting the answer in seconds!

Why It Matters:
Businesses save time, reduce costs, and improve customer satisfaction.

3. Automating Workflows: AI as Your Digital Assistant

AI doesn't just help with big decisions; it also makes daily tasks faster and smoother by automating workflows.

- **What Is Workflow Automation?**
Imagine you're running a business. Every day, you:

  - Process invoices.
  - Schedule meetings.
  - Send emails to customers.

These repetitive tasks take up valuable time. AI automates them so you can focus on bigger, more important work.

Examples of Workflow Automation:

- **Invoice Processing**: AI tools scan and process invoices automatically, saving hours of manual data entry.
- **Email Automation**: AI tools like Mailchimp or HubSpot send personalized emails to customers based on their behavior.
- **Scheduling Meetings**: Tools like Calendly use AI to coordinate schedules without endless back-and-forth emails.

Why It Matters:

- Businesses become **faster** and **more efficient**.

- Employees spend less time on repetitive tasks and more on creative, strategic work.

4. AI in Marketing: Creating Better Content and Campaigns

Here's where things get exciting: Generative AI has revolutionized **marketing**. From writing ads to creating social media posts, AI is becoming a marketer's best friend.

- **Content Creation**:
  Tools like ChatGPT and Jasper generate blog posts, marketing emails, and even ad copy in seconds. For example:

  - You need a blog post on "Top 5 Benefits of Yoga for Stress Relief"? AI can generate a full draft for you.
  - Need 10 catchy captions for Instagram? AI delivers ideas instantly.

- **Personalized Marketing**:
  AI tools analyze customer data to create personalized marketing campaigns. For instance:

  - If a customer often buys running shoes, AI recommends fitness-related products in their emails.

- **Ad Optimization**:
  AI platforms like Google Ads analyze which ads perform best and adjust campaigns automatically for better results.

Real-World Example:

- Netflix uses AI to recommend movies based on what you've watched. That's marketing personalization at its finest!

5. AI in Data Analysis: Unlocking Business Insights

Businesses collect data from everywhere—sales numbers, customer reviews, website traffic, and more. But what does all this data mean? AI tools help businesses:

- **Analyze data faster**.

- **Visualize insights clearly** (through charts and dashboards).
- **Predict future trends** (like customer behavior or market demand).

Example:

- A clothing brand uses AI to analyze customer reviews. AI finds that many customers mention "size issues." The brand can now fix its sizing problems to improve customer satisfaction.

Tools That Help:

- **Power BI**, **Tableau**, and AI-powered **Google Analytics** help businesses make sense of complex data quickly.

6. Real-World Success Stories: AI-Powered Businesses

Let's look at a few examples of companies leveraging AI to achieve massive success:

- **Amazon**: Uses AI for everything—personalized product recommendations, inventory management, and delivery route optimization.
- **Spotify**: Analyzes listening habits to suggest music and create personalized playlists like *Discover Weekly*.
- **Starbucks**: Uses AI to predict customer orders and recommend items based on the time of day, weather, or past purchases.

These businesses are proof that AI is not just for tech companies—it's for *everyone*.

7. Why Generative AI Is the Game-Changer

What makes **Generative AI** stand out in business is its ability to *create*.

- AI can **generate content**—like blog posts, ads, or videos—saving businesses time and money.
- AI can **simulate scenarios**—like predicting how customers will respond to a new product launch.
- AI helps **brainstorm creative ideas**, offering businesses fresh perspectives.

Imagine running a small business. You need:

- A blog post to attract customers.
- Social media posts to build a following.
- Personalized email campaigns to boost sales.

Generative AI tools do all of this in minutes, even if you're not a writer or designer.

Final Thoughts: AI as a Business Superpower

AI and Generative AI are no longer buzzwords—they are business essentials. From analyzing data to serving customers, automating tasks, and creating content, AI is helping businesses of all sizes work smarter and faster.

If you're running a business, think of AI as your *superpower*. It won't replace you or your team; instead, it will help you make better decisions, unlock creativity, and serve customers like never before.

Are you ready to embrace AI in your business? The future of work isn't about working harder—it's about working *smarter*.

XXII

Generative AI in Education

"Education is the passport to the future, and with AI, we're giving students the tools to unlock it faster and smarter."

Imagine a classroom where every student gets individual attention, lessons adapt to their learning pace, assignments are generated instantly, and even teachers get a digital assistant to help them out. No, this isn't a scene from a sci-fi movie—this is how **Generative AI** is transforming education right now.

Education has always been about empowerment, knowledge, and creativity. But let's be honest—students and teachers often face challenges like:

- One-size-fits-all learning that doesn't suit everyone.
- Limited time for teachers to give personalized feedback.
- Huge workloads, like grading, planning, and creating content.

Generative AI is stepping in as the ultimate helper. From personalized learning paths for students to research and academic publishing, AI is revolutionizing how we teach, learn, and discover. Let's explore how this works, without any tech jargon—just real-world examples that you can relate to!

1. Personalized Learning with AI and Generative Tools

Have you ever noticed how *Netflix* recommends movies or shows based on what you like? Imagine if education worked the same way—lessons tailored to each student's strengths, weaknesses, and interests. That's what **AI-powered personalized learning** does.

- **What is Personalized Learning?**
It's the idea that every student learns differently. Instead of forcing everyone to follow the same syllabus at the same speed, AI tools adapt to individual needs.

How AI Does It:

- AI analyzes a student's performance, learning style, and pace.
- It then adjusts the difficulty of lessons, provides extra practice for weaker areas, and speeds up topics a student already knows.

Example in Action:

- **Khan Academy's AI Tutor**: Platforms like Khan Academy use AI to create a "tutor experience." If a student struggles with fractions, the AI will suggest extra practice problems and videos that explain concepts step-by-step.
- **Duolingo**: Learning a new language? Duolingo's AI adapts questions to match your skill level. If you keep making mistakes on Spanish verb tenses, it'll focus on improving that area.

Why It Matters:

- Students learn at their own pace—no one feels left behind.
- It keeps learning engaging and less frustrating.

Imagine a child who struggles with math but loves science. With AI, their math lessons are tailored to build confidence while allowing them to dive deeper into science topics they're passionate about. That's the magic of personalized learning.

2. AI-Powered Educational Assistants

Teachers often have too much on their plates—planning lessons, grading assignments, answering questions, and more. AI-powered **educational**

assistants step in to ease their workload and allow teachers to focus on what truly matters: **teaching and inspiring students**.

What Educational Assistants Do:

- **Automate Grading**: AI tools like Gradescope grade multiple-choice quizzes, essays, and assignments in minutes. No more late-night grading marathons for teachers!
- **Answer Common Questions**: AI-powered bots can answer frequently asked student queries like, *"What's the homework for today?"* or *"How do I solve this equation?"*
- **Generate Lesson Plans**: AI tools can draft lesson plans, worksheets, and tests based on specific topics or standards.

Example in Action:

- **ChatGPT as a Teaching Assistant**: Imagine a history teacher wants to create questions for a quiz about World War II. Instead of spending hours brainstorming, they ask ChatGPT, *"Generate 10 quiz questions on WWII,"* and—voila!—the questions are ready in seconds.
- **AI Tools for Feedback**: Tools like Grammarly provide instant feedback on students' writing, pointing out grammar errors, style improvements, and better word choices.

Why It Matters:

- Teachers save time and reduce stress.
- Students get faster feedback, which helps them learn and improve.

3. Adaptive Learning Systems: Learning Made Smarter

If personalized learning is about tailoring lessons to individuals, **adaptive learning systems** take it a step further. These AI systems constantly "learn" about the student and adapt in real-time.

How It Works:

- AI tracks how students perform on quizzes, practice tests, and assignments.
- If a student excels in algebra but struggles with geometry, the AI adjusts lessons to focus on geometry.

Real-World Example:

- **DreamBox**: A math learning platform for kids. DreamBox adapts lessons based on how the child interacts with the problems. If they breeze through addition, it'll move to multiplication. If they get stuck, it'll break the problem into smaller, easier steps.

Why It Matters:

- Adaptive learning makes lessons **dynamic** instead of rigid.
- Students stay engaged because they're always learning at a comfortable level.

4. AI and Generative Tools for Content Creation

Creating educational content—like lesson plans, study guides, and question papers—takes time. Generative AI tools help teachers and educators do this faster and better.

- **Lesson Plans**: Teachers can use AI to generate lesson plans for any subject in seconds.
  Example: *"Create a lesson plan for Grade 8 about the solar system."* AI drafts topics, activities, and even homework assignments!
- **Study Guides and Notes**: AI can summarize long textbooks into easy-to-read study notes.
  Example: Tools like ChatGPT or Perplexity AI summarize chapters into key points so students can revise faster.
- **Quizzes and Tests**: Generative AI creates questions for quizzes or mock exams.
  Example: Teachers can ask AI to generate 20 questions on Shakespeare's *Macbeth*—multiple-choice, short answers, or essays.

Why It Matters:

- Teachers save hours on planning and content creation.
- Students get high-quality, tailored study materials.

5. AI in Research, Writing, and Academic Publishing

AI is not just for classrooms; it's also revolutionizing **academic research and writing**.

- **Research Made Easy**: AI tools like Semantic Scholar or ResearchRabbit help researchers find papers, studies, and references faster by analyzing massive academic databases.
- **Writing and Editing**: AI tools like Grammarly, QuillBot, and ChatGPT assist in writing research papers, essays, or dissertations by suggesting edits, rephrasing content, and improving clarity.
- **Plagiarism Detection**: Tools like Turnitin use AI to check if students' work is original or copied.

Real-World Impact:

- Researchers spend less time looking for papers and formatting content, and more time **discovering new ideas**.
- Students write better, clearer essays with AI-powered guidance.

6. Real-World Success Stories

Let's take a quick look at how AI is already transforming education worldwide:

- **India**: EdTech platforms like BYJU's and Vedantu use AI to provide personalized online classes to millions of students.
- **USA**: Tools like Quizlet use AI to help students memorize concepts faster through flashcards and adaptive quizzes.
- **Global Universities**: Institutions like MIT and Stanford are integrating AI into classrooms to enhance research and learning.

Final Thoughts: AI—the Future of Education

Generative AI is not here to replace teachers or traditional learning—it's here to make education **smarter, faster, and more accessible** for everyone.

- Students get personalized support.
- Teachers save time with content creation and grading.
- Researchers uncover ideas faster.

Education is no longer confined to textbooks and chalkboards; it's evolving into an intelligent, dynamic experience that adapts to each learner's needs.

So, whether you're a student struggling with algebra or a teacher juggling lesson plans, AI is your ally.

The future of learning isn't about replacing human educators—it's about empowering them to create a better, brighter future for learners everywhere.

XXIII

AI and Healthcare

Have you ever wondered how doctors predict illnesses, analyze complex scans, or discover new treatments? Behind many medical breakthroughs today lies an invisible helping hand: **Artificial Intelligence (AI).**

AI is revolutionizing healthcare. From identifying diseases earlier than ever before to tailoring treatment plans for individuals, AI is working alongside doctors to save lives. It's like having a team of tireless medical experts—who never need sleep—analyzing mountains of data, finding patterns, and helping make life-changing decisions.

In this chapter, we'll dive into the fascinating world of AI in healthcare. Don't worry—we'll keep the medical and technical jargon simple so anyone can understand. Let's explore how AI is helping patients, doctors, and researchers reshape the future of medicine!

1. AI in Diagnostics: Spotting Illness Before It's Too Late

When we visit a doctor, they often rely on tests, scans, and observations to diagnose what's wrong. But what if AI could analyze this data much faster and more accurately, catching diseases in their early stages when they're easier to treat? That's exactly what's happening.

AI-Powered Medical Imaging

Imagine a doctor staring at an X-ray or an MRI scan. A small tumor or fracture could be easy to miss, especially in its early stages. AI tools, powered by generative models, can scan thousands of images in seconds and highlight even the tiniest abnormality.

Real-World Example:

- **Google's DeepMind**: Their AI models can analyze eye scans to detect diabetic retinopathy (a condition caused by diabetes that can lead to blindness) with accuracy matching top ophthalmologists.
- **Lung Cancer Detection**: AI systems like those by IBM Watson and GE Healthcare help spot early signs of lung cancer in CT scans, sometimes detecting things that human eyes might overlook.

How It Works:

- AI systems are trained on thousands (even millions) of medical images, like X-rays or MRIs.
- Over time, the AI "learns" to identify patterns that indicate a disease or condition.
- Doctors then use these AI insights to confirm diagnoses and make informed decisions.

Why It Matters:

- Early diagnosis = better chances of treatment and recovery.
- Doctors get AI support, reducing the risk of human errors in critical cases.

2. Predictive Medicine: Forecasting Illness Before It Happens

Wouldn't it be great if we could predict illnesses before they occur? With AI, this isn't a dream—it's reality. AI tools can analyze a patient's medical history, genetic data, and even lifestyle habits to predict the likelihood of developing certain diseases.

What is Predictive Medicine?

It's like having a crystal ball for your health. AI tools study patterns in your data to predict the future risks of diseases like diabetes, heart disease, or cancer.

Real-World Example:

- **AI for Heart Disease**: Platforms like Cardiologs analyze ECG (heart activity) data to predict the risk of heart attacks or arrhythmias before they become life-threatening.
- **Wearable Technology**: Devices like smartwatches use AI to track your heart rate, activity, and sleep. They send alerts if they detect unusual patterns, such as a dangerously high heart rate.

How AI Does It:

- AI studies large datasets of patient histories.
- It identifies trends—like symptoms, genetics, or habits—that typically lead to illnesses.
- Doctors then use this analysis to recommend lifestyle changes, medications, or preventive care.

Why It Matters:

- Patients can take action **before** a disease develops.
- Healthcare shifts from reactive (treating illnesses) to **proactive** (preventing illnesses).

3. Personalized Treatment Plans: Medicine Tailored for You

Not everyone responds to treatments in the same way. What works for one patient may not work for another. That's where AI steps in to create **personalized treatment plans** based on your unique health data.

How Does It Work?

AI combines your medical history, genetic data, and even real-time health stats to design a treatment specifically for you.

Real-World Example:

- **Cancer Treatment**: Platforms like IBM Watson for Oncology analyze thousands of cancer cases and research papers. They recommend customized treatment options based on the patient's specific cancer type and genetic makeup.
- **Precision Medicine**: AI tools help doctors select medications that are most likely to work for a particular patient, reducing the trial-and-error process.

Why It Matters:

- Treatments become **more effective** and cause fewer side effects.
- Patients get care tailored to their unique needs.

4. Generative AI in Medical Research and Drug Discovery

Developing new medicines can take **years** of research and testing. AI is speeding up this process. Generative AI models can analyze scientific data and even help design new drugs faster than humans.

How AI Accelerates Drug Discovery

- AI scans through massive medical databases and research papers to identify molecules or compounds that could fight a disease.
- Generative AI then simulates how these compounds might work, helping scientists narrow down the best options for testing.

Real-World Example:

- **Insilico Medicine**: They used AI to identify a new drug candidate for treating fibrosis in just 46 days—something that usually takes months or years.

- **AI in COVID-19**: During the pandemic, AI was used to study how the virus spreads, develop vaccines faster, and identify drugs that could treat symptoms.

Why It Matters:

- Faster drug discovery = more lives saved.
- Medical breakthroughs become more affordable and accessible.

5. Ethical Issues and Privacy Concerns

While AI is transforming healthcare, it also raises some important ethical questions:

1. **Bias in AI**:

   - AI models are only as good as the data they're trained on. If the data isn't diverse, the AI might give biased results.
   - Example: An AI model trained only on data from one country might not work as well for patients in other regions.

2. **Privacy and Security**:

   - Healthcare involves sensitive personal data. AI tools must protect this information from breaches or misuse.
   - Patients need assurance that their medical data is safe and won't be used without consent.

3. **Decision-Making**:

   - Should AI make life-or-death decisions, like whether a patient needs surgery? While AI can assist, the final call should always be made by human doctors.

Final Thoughts: AI—the Doctor's New Best Friend

AI is not replacing doctors; it's **augmenting their capabilities**. With AI:

- Diagnoses are faster and more accurate.
- Treatments are more personalized and effective.
- Research is speeding up to bring new cures to the world.

Imagine a future where no disease goes undetected, where doctors can focus on human care while AI handles the data, and where patients receive treatments made just for them. That future isn't decades away—it's happening right now.

"AI in healthcare is not just about technology; it's about hope. It's about saving lives, improving health, and giving us all the chance to live longer, healthier lives."

XXIV

AI and Generative AI in Finance

In this chapter, we'll explore how AI and Generative AI are revolutionizing the world of finance. From streamlining banking processes to predicting stock market trends, AI has become the backbone of the modern financial ecosystem. Whether you're a casual investor, a banking professional, or just curious about how AI impacts your wallet, this chapter will help you understand how technology is driving financial innovation.

The Financial World Gets Smarter

Imagine this: You're opening a new bank account online. A chatbot seamlessly guides you through every step, ensures your details are correct, and verifies your identity within minutes. That's AI at work!

Or let's say you're curious about investing in stocks. Instead of manually researching endless market data, an AI-powered tool analyzes trends, risk factors, and historical data to recommend the best options tailored to your needs.

AI in finance is **not just about speed**; it's about precision, personalization, and creating smarter financial systems.

Key Applications of AI and Generative AI in Finance

Let's break down where AI and Generative AI are making waves in the financial sector.

1. Fraud Detection and Risk Management

Fraud in the financial sector is a major concern, but AI is fighting back!

- **How does it work?** AI uses advanced algorithms to analyze massive volumes of financial transactions in real time. If it detects any unusual activity—like a sudden, large withdrawal or purchases from an unexpected location—it flags the transaction immediately.
- **Generative AI's role:** Generative AI can simulate various fraud scenarios to train fraud detection systems to be more proactive and accurate.

Example: Banks like **HDFC** and **ICICI** in India are already leveraging AI tools to monitor fraudulent activities and reduce risks for their customers.

2. Personalized Banking and Customer Experience

Have you ever noticed how your banking app or website now knows exactly what you need?

- AI enables banks to create **personalized experiences** for their customers. From suggesting customized financial plans to answering queries via chatbots, AI ensures your banking needs are met efficiently.
- **Generative AI in chatbots:** Tools like ChatGPT-like bots are being deployed in banks to interact with customers in a conversational, human-like manner, helping with loan inquiries, account updates, and even financial planning.

Example: Virtual assistants such as **SBI's YONO** or **Axis Bank's Aha!** streamline customer interactions through AI-driven insights.

3. Stock Market Predictions and Algorithmic Trading

The stock market is complex, volatile, and often unpredictable. However, AI is now being used to analyze data, detect trends, and make predictions that investors can act on.

- **AI algorithms** can process massive amounts of market data within seconds—something human analysts could never achieve on their own.
- **Algorithmic trading** powered by AI helps execute trades automatically based on pre-set rules and real-time market data.

Generative AI's role: Generative AI can simulate market behaviors under different scenarios, helping analysts and investors test strategies before risking real capital.

Example: Global financial giants like **Goldman Sachs** use AI to enhance their trading capabilities. In India, **Zerodha** and **Upstox** integrate AI tools to help retail investors make smarter decisions.

4. Credit Scoring and Loan Approvals

Getting a loan approved used to take days (or weeks), but AI has transformed the process.

- **AI-driven credit scoring** analyzes a borrower's financial history, spending behavior, and other data points to determine creditworthiness instantly.
- Lenders use AI to make fairer, faster, and more accurate decisions.

Generative AI's role: Generative AI can simulate risk assessments, helping lenders understand how different loan portfolios might behave over time.

Example: Fintech companies like **Bajaj Finserv** and **LendingKart** use AI to approve loans in hours, particularly for small businesses in Tier 2 and Tier 3 cities in India.

5. Financial Forecasting and Budgeting

AI is helping businesses and individuals forecast future financial needs and plan budgets effectively.

- AI tools analyze past financial data, identify trends, and predict future income, expenses, or investments.
- **Generative AI** can generate hypothetical budget scenarios to prepare organizations for unexpected challenges like market crashes or economic slowdowns.

Example: Apps like **Walnut** or **Moneycontrol** use AI to provide personalized budgeting and financial advice.

The Role of AI in Financial Inclusion

One of the most exciting impacts of AI and Generative AI in finance is **financial inclusion.** In India, where millions of people live in rural areas without access to traditional banks, AI-powered fintech solutions are bridging the gap.

- Digital wallets like **Paytm, Google Pay, and PhonePe** use AI to help even those without formal bank accounts make transactions.
- AI chatbots available in local languages (including Telugu, Hindi, and Marathi) make financial services accessible to the masses.

Example: AI-driven **UPI payments** have revolutionized how small shopkeepers, farmers, and daily wage workers handle their finances.

Challenges of AI in Finance

While the possibilities are endless, AI in finance isn't without challenges:

1. **Bias in AI models:** AI can sometimes make decisions based on biased data, leading to unfair loan denials or inaccurate predictions.
2. **Privacy concerns:** Financial data is sensitive, and AI systems need strong security to prevent misuse.
3. **Dependence on data:** Without clean, high-quality data, AI predictions and insights may fail.

To address these challenges, responsible AI use, ethical standards, and regulatory frameworks are critical.

Looking Ahead: The Future of Finance with AI

As AI continues to evolve, the future of finance will see even more personalized, automated, and efficient systems.

- AI could create entirely autonomous financial advisors.
- Blockchain technology and AI might combine to improve transparency and security.
- Generative AI may build fully simulated financial markets to test global economic models.

"**A Thought:** *Imagine a world where AI helps every individual in India—from a student in Hyderabad to a farmer in Tamil Nadu—access fair and transparent financial services. That's the* *potential we're headed toward.*"

AI and Generative AI are not just transforming the financial sector—they're redefining how we interact with money itself. From fraud detection to personalized investment advice, these technologies are empowering businesses, individuals, and economies.

XXV

AI in Cybersecurity

As we move deeper into the digital age, the world is becoming more connected—and more vulnerable. Every click, login, or swipe leaves a digital footprint, and cybercriminals are constantly looking for ways to exploit these trails. Whether it's hacking into personal accounts, stealing sensitive information, or launching large-scale attacks on corporations, cybersecurity is now more important than ever.

But here's the good news: **AI is stepping up as a digital bodyguard**, fighting threats faster and smarter than humans ever could. In this chapter, we'll explore how AI is revolutionizing cybersecurity and keeping our digital world safe.

Why Cybersecurity Needs AI

Let's begin with a simple question: **Why can't humans handle cybersecurity on their own?**

The answer lies in **scale and speed**.

1. **Massive Data Volumes**: Millions of cyber events happen every day—far too many for humans to track.
2. **Evolving Threats**: Cyberattacks are becoming more complex, with new malware and hacking strategies appearing almost daily.
3. **Speed of Response**: Cyberattacks often happen in real time, and any delay can cause massive damage.

This is where **Artificial Intelligence (AI)** comes in. AI can process enormous amounts of data in seconds, detect hidden patterns, and act immediately to prevent damage.

Think of it like this: If a human is a security guard with a flashlight, AI is a **high-tech security system with cameras, sensors, and predictive tools** working all at once.

How AI is Transforming Cybersecurity

Here are some of the key ways AI is playing a leading role in cybersecurity:

1. Threat Detection and Prevention

The first step in cybersecurity is detecting threats—and AI does it faster and more accurately than humans.

- **How it works**: AI systems analyze huge amounts of data to identify unusual patterns. For example, if a user suddenly logs in from an unknown location or downloads a suspicious file, AI flags this activity as a potential threat.
- **Machine learning** allows these systems to continuously learn and improve, becoming better at spotting new types of attacks.

Example:

Many banks and financial organizations use AI to detect fraudulent transactions. If you've ever received a notification asking, *"Was this you?"*, it's likely AI spotted something unusual about that transaction.

2. AI-Powered Firewalls and Antivirus Software

Traditional firewalls and antivirus programs often rely on pre-existing data about known threats. However, cybercriminals are always inventing new techniques.

- AI-powered systems go a step further. They can detect **unknown threats** by analyzing behaviors rather than relying solely on known patterns.
- AI continuously monitors system activity and can automatically block suspicious actions in real time.

Example:

AI-driven security tools like **Darktrace** and **CrowdStrike** use real-time analysis to prevent attacks before they occur.

3. Predictive Analysis and Proactive Defense

Imagine if you could predict a cyberattack before it happens—that's exactly what AI does.

- AI analyzes data to predict potential vulnerabilities and warn companies about **where and how they might be attacked**.
- By simulating different cyberattack scenarios, AI helps organizations fix weak points before hackers can exploit them.

Real-Life Use Case:

Companies often run **penetration tests** using AI to check for gaps in their systems. Think of it like hiring a friendly "hacker" to identify weak spots so you can lock them down.

4. Automating Incident Response

When a cyberattack happens, every second counts. Instead of waiting for humans to investigate, AI can respond instantly.

- AI systems automatically isolate infected parts of a network to stop the attack from spreading.
- Some AI tools even generate **detailed reports** to help security teams understand what happened and how to prevent it in the future.

Example:

Large companies like **Microsoft** and **IBM** use AI to automate their response to cyber incidents, reducing downtime and preventing widespread damage.

5. Fighting Phishing and Social Engineering Attacks

Phishing emails are one of the most common forms of cyberattacks. Ever received an email saying, *"Your bank account has been locked. Click here to verify!"*? That's phishing in action.

- AI tools use **natural language processing (NLP)** to analyze email content and detect phishing attempts.
- AI can spot unusual phrasing, fake links, or impersonated email addresses that a human might miss.

Example:

Many email providers like **Gmail** now use AI to filter out phishing emails and protect users.

6. Securing the Internet of Things (IoT)

Our homes, cars, and workplaces are now full of "smart" devices—everything from security cameras to refrigerators. But these devices can also be hacked if not secured properly.

- AI helps monitor and secure IoT devices by detecting abnormal activities, like a smart fridge suddenly trying to access your banking app.
- AI can automatically cut off compromised devices to protect the rest of the network.

Generative AI in Cybersecurity

Generative AI is not just for art and text; it's also becoming a powerful tool for cybersecurity.

1. **Simulating Attacks**: Generative AI can simulate various types of cyberattacks, helping organizations train their systems to respond effectively.
2. **Creating Defense Tools**: Generative models can design advanced security patches to fix vulnerabilities in software.

However, generative AI also poses risks, as cybercriminals can use it to:

- Create sophisticated phishing emails.
- Generate malware that can bypass traditional defenses.

This is why **ethical AI use** is more important than ever.

Challenges in AI Cybersecurity

While AI is a game-changer, it's not perfect. Here are a few challenges:

1. **Adversarial Attacks**: Hackers can "trick" AI systems by feeding them manipulated data.
2. **Data Privacy**: AI relies on data, but ensuring this data is secure and private can be a challenge.

3. **Cost**: Implementing AI-powered cybersecurity tools can be expensive for small businesses.

Organizations need to balance AI's power with ethical considerations and robust safeguards.

Looking to the Future

The future of cybersecurity will be an ongoing race between attackers and defenders. AI will continue to evolve, providing even smarter and faster defenses.

- We'll see more **AI-driven security ecosystems**, where tools work together to provide holistic protection.
- AI could create **autonomous cyber "police" systems** to monitor and secure the entire internet.
- Collaboration between governments, companies, and individuals will be key to building a safer digital world.

AI in cybersecurity is not just about defending against threats—it's about building trust in our digital lives. Whether you're making an online payment, using a smart device, or running a company, AI is silently working in the background to keep you safe.

The digital world is vast, complex, and full of opportunities, but it's also full of risks. With AI as our strongest ally, we can build a safer, smarter future where technology empowers us without compromising our security.

XXVI

AI in Government and Policy

When you think about Artificial Intelligence, your mind might jump to robots, virtual assistants, or creative AI tools, but **AI has a powerful role to play in government and policymaking as well.** In fact, AI is already transforming the way governments operate, improving public services, policymaking, and even national security.

In this chapter, we'll explore how governments around the world are adopting AI to solve real-world problems, make better decisions, and serve citizens more effectively.

Why Governments Need AI

Governments handle massive amounts of data and are responsible for solving some of society's biggest challenges—think healthcare, education, infrastructure, and security. But here's the problem:

1. **Data Overload**: The sheer volume of data is overwhelming for humans to analyze.
2. **Complex Decision-Making**: Policymakers need to make decisions that impact millions, often in a short amount of time.
3. **Resource Constraints**: Limited manpower and resources make it difficult to address issues efficiently.

This is where AI steps in. By analyzing data, predicting trends, and automating tasks, AI allows governments to **work smarter, faster, and more efficiently**.

Imagine AI as a super-assistant for governments—helping to spot problems, suggest solutions, and improve outcomes for citizens.

AI in Public Services

Let's start with one of the most visible areas of AI in government: **public services**.

1. Smart Cities

AI plays a major role in creating "smart cities"—urban areas that use technology to improve quality of life.

- **Traffic Management**: AI systems analyze real-time traffic data to reduce congestion, optimize traffic lights, and even suggest alternative routes.
- **Waste Management**: AI helps track waste levels in cities and deploy resources efficiently to keep areas clean.
- **Energy Efficiency**: AI optimizes electricity use by analyzing consumption patterns and managing smart grids.

Example: In Singapore, AI systems monitor traffic and adjust signals dynamically, reducing traffic jams and saving commuters time.

2. Healthcare and Social Services

Governments use AI to provide better healthcare and social welfare services.

- **AI in Healthcare**: AI-powered tools help hospitals manage patient data, detect diseases, and predict health trends.
- **Social Welfare**: AI analyzes data to ensure benefits are delivered to the right people and detect fraud in welfare programs.

Example: In the UK, the National Health Service (NHS) uses AI to predict which patients are at higher risk of hospital readmission, allowing for preventive care.

3. Education and Skill Development

AI helps governments improve education systems and prepare citizens for the jobs of the future.

- **Personalized Learning**: AI tools create customized learning plans for students based on their abilities and progress.
- **Skill Gap Analysis**: Governments use AI to identify skill gaps in the workforce and design programs to address them.

Example: India's AI-powered education programs use adaptive learning to provide equal opportunities to students in remote areas.

AI in Policymaking

Policymaking often requires analyzing vast amounts of information and predicting how policies will impact society. AI helps governments make better decisions by:

1. Data-Driven Decisions

AI analyzes economic, social, and environmental data to offer insights that guide policy.

- Governments can use AI to predict trends such as unemployment rates, poverty levels, or environmental changes.
- Policymakers can simulate the effects of different policies before implementing them.

Example: In the United States, AI tools analyze economic data to help shape policies related to employment, inflation, and taxation.

2. Predictive Governance

AI helps governments anticipate problems and solve them before they become bigger issues.

- **Disaster Management**: AI predicts natural disasters like floods or hurricanes, enabling governments to issue early warnings and evacuate people.
- **Crime Prevention**: AI-powered tools analyze crime data to identify high-risk areas and allocate police resources efficiently.

Example: Japan uses AI to predict earthquakes and tsunamis, giving residents enough time to evacuate and stay safe.

AI in National Security and Defense

National security is a top priority for any government, and AI is playing an increasingly critical role in protecting citizens.

- **Surveillance and Threat Detection**: AI systems monitor and analyze large amounts of security data to detect suspicious activities or potential attacks.
- **Cybersecurity**: Governments use AI to protect critical infrastructure from cyberattacks and defend against digital threats.
- **Defense Automation**: AI supports military operations through autonomous drones, predictive intelligence, and automated logistics.

Example: Israel uses AI-based surveillance tools to monitor border security and prevent infiltration.

Challenges and Ethical Concerns

While AI can significantly improve governance, it also comes with challenges:

1. Data Privacy

AI systems require large amounts of citizen data, which raises concerns about how this data is collected, stored, and used.

- Citizens worry about surveillance and loss of privacy.

2. Bias and Fairness

AI models can sometimes reflect biases present in their training data. If not managed, these biases could lead to unfair decisions.

- For example, biased AI systems might deny welfare benefits to certain groups unfairly.

3. Transparency and Trust

AI decisions can often feel like a "black box"—where we don't fully understand how the system reached its conclusion.

- Governments must ensure transparency in AI systems to build public trust.

AI Regulations and Global Initiatives

To address these concerns, many countries are working on AI regulations and frameworks:

- **The European Union**: The EU's AI Act aims to ensure AI is used safely, ethically, and transparently.
- **United Nations**: The UN is exploring global guidelines for responsible AI use.
- **Country-Specific Regulations**: Countries like the US, China, and India are creating policies to balance AI innovation with ethical considerations.

Governments are also collaborating with tech companies and researchers to ensure AI benefits everyone.

The Future of AI in Government

The role of AI in governance is only going to grow. Here's what the future might hold:

1. **AI-Driven Policy Simulations**: Governments will use AI to simulate policies and predict long-term impacts.
2. **AI for Global Issues**: AI will help tackle climate change, poverty, and global health crises.
3. **Citizen-Focused AI**: AI systems will be more transparent, user-friendly, and focused on improving citizen welfare.

Imagine a world where governments can respond to emergencies faster, eliminate corruption, and deliver services that are perfectly tailored to every citizen's needs—all powered by AI.

AI in government and policy isn't just about machines taking over—it's about making better decisions, solving complex problems, and improving lives. From public services to national security, AI is helping governments create a more efficient, responsive, and inclusive future.

As citizens, understanding how AI shapes our governments gives us the power to ask questions, demand transparency, and ensure AI is used responsibly.

XXVII

AI for Sustainability and the Environment

As we face the growing challenges of climate change, pollution, and the depletion of natural resources, AI is emerging as a powerful tool in the fight for a sustainable future. From predicting climate patterns to optimizing energy use, AI is reshaping how we approach environmental conservation, resource management, and climate action.

In this chapter, we'll explore how AI is helping us make smarter, greener choices and creating a more sustainable world for future generations.

Why AI for Sustainability?

Sustainability refers to the responsible use and management of resources to meet the needs of the present without compromising the ability of future generations to meet their own needs. This includes managing natural resources, reducing pollution, and mitigating the effects of climate change.

But tackling sustainability challenges requires intelligent, data-driven solutions—something AI is well-equipped to provide. AI systems can analyze vast amounts of environmental data, predict trends, and help us make better decisions to protect the planet.

Let's dive into some of the key areas where AI is driving positive change.

AI in Climate Change Prediction and Mitigation

One of the most pressing issues humanity faces today is **climate change**. The science is clear: human activities, especially the burning of fossil fuels, are contributing to global warming and extreme weather events. But AI is helping us better understand climate patterns and find ways to reduce greenhouse gas emissions.

1. Climate Modeling and Forecasting

AI is used to model complex climate systems and predict how they will evolve. These models help scientists understand potential future scenarios, such as rising sea levels, temperature changes, and more frequent natural disasters.

- **Climate Modeling**: AI algorithms analyze historical climate data and simulate how different factors (like emissions or deforestation) will impact future climate patterns.
- **Extreme Weather Prediction**: AI can also predict extreme weather events, such as hurricanes, droughts, or floods, giving governments and communities time to prepare and respond.

Example: The **IBM Green Horizons** initiative uses AI to create predictive models of air quality and weather, helping cities like Beijing reduce pollution and improve public health.

2. Carbon Footprint Reduction

To tackle climate change, we need to reduce the amount of carbon dioxide (CO_2) and other greenhouse gases we emit. AI is playing a critical role in **monitoring, reducing, and offsetting emissions.**

- **Carbon Tracking**: AI helps businesses and governments track their carbon emissions in real time, identify areas where emissions can be reduced, and monitor progress toward sustainability goals.
- **Sustainable Practices**: AI can optimize manufacturing processes, supply chains, and energy use to lower carbon footprints and promote more sustainable practices.

Example: AI is helping companies like **Microsoft** reduce their emissions by optimizing energy usage across their data centers and infrastructure.

AI in Renewable Energy

Transitioning to **renewable energy** is a cornerstone of sustainability. Solar, wind, and hydroelectric power are key sources of clean energy, but they come with their own challenges. AI is helping overcome these challenges by improving energy generation, storage, and distribution.

1. Smart Grids

A smart grid is an energy network that uses AI to monitor and control the flow of electricity. AI algorithms analyze data from power plants, energy storage systems, and consumers to optimize energy distribution in real-time. This results in more efficient use of renewable energy sources and reduces waste.

- **Energy Distribution**: AI helps balance supply and demand by predicting energy needs and adjusting power generation accordingly.
- **Renewable Energy Integration**: AI improves the integration of renewable energy sources, such as solar and wind, into the grid by forecasting energy generation based on weather patterns.

Example: **Google** has developed AI tools to optimize the operation of solar farms, improving the efficiency of solar energy production.

2. Energy Efficiency

AI can also help homes, businesses, and industries reduce their energy consumption. By analyzing usage patterns, AI systems can provide real-time feedback and recommendations for energy-saving actions.

- **Smart Homes**: AI-powered smart thermostats and appliances learn from user behavior to adjust energy use, making homes more energy-efficient.
- **Industrial Efficiency**: AI helps factories and industrial facilities optimize processes to reduce waste and energy consumption.

Example: **Nest Thermostats** use AI to learn your home's temperature preferences and adjust heating or cooling schedules, reducing energy consumption while maintaining comfort.

AI in Wildlife Conservation and Biodiversity

Our planet is home to a stunning array of species, but many are facing threats from habitat loss, poaching, and climate change. AI is being used to monitor wildlife populations, track endangered species, and prevent illegal activities.

1. Wildlife Monitoring

AI-powered cameras, drones, and sensors are helping conservationists monitor wildlife populations in remote areas. These systems can track animal movements, identify species, and even detect health risks in populations.

- **Wildlife Tracking**: AI analyzes data from drones and satellites to track animal migrations and habitat changes.
- **Poaching Prevention**: AI systems can identify suspicious activity in protected areas, such as poaching or illegal logging, by analyzing patterns in data.

Example: The **Elephant Listening Project** in Africa uses AI to analyze audio data from microphones placed in forests to track elephant populations and detect illegal poaching activities.

AI in Agriculture and Food Security

Agriculture is critical to feeding the world's growing population, but it also has a significant environmental impact. AI is helping farmers improve yields, reduce water usage, and decrease pesticide dependence, all while minimizing environmental harm.

1. Precision Agriculture

AI can analyze soil health, weather patterns, and crop data to help farmers make better decisions about planting, irrigation, and harvesting. By using AI, farmers can optimize resource use and reduce waste.

- **Water Management**: AI monitors soil moisture levels to determine when and how much water crops need, reducing water waste.
- **Pest Control**: AI systems can detect signs of pests and diseases early, allowing farmers to take action before these problems spread.

Example: Companies like **John Deere** are using AI-powered tractors and harvesters that can plant seeds, apply fertilizers, and harvest crops with minimal human intervention, making farming more efficient and environmentally friendly.

AI in Waste Management and Recycling

Managing waste and recycling efficiently is another key challenge for sustainability. AI can help optimize waste collection, recycling processes, and reduce landfill waste.

1. Smart Waste Management

AI helps cities improve waste collection by analyzing waste patterns and optimizing collection routes. By knowing where waste is accumulating, cities can reduce fuel consumption and improve efficiency.

- **Recycling Sorting**: AI can automatically sort recyclable materials from waste, ensuring that valuable resources are reused and reducing contamination.
- **Waste-to-Energy**: AI optimizes the process of converting waste into energy, reducing landfill waste and providing a cleaner energy source.

Example: **ZenRobotics** in Finland has developed AI-powered robotic systems that automatically sort construction waste, ensuring that reusable materials are separated from trash.

Challenges and the Road Ahead

While AI offers immense potential for sustainability, it is not without its challenges:

- **Data Availability**: High-quality, accurate data is essential for training AI systems. In many cases, data on environmental issues is scarce or fragmented.
- **Bias and Fairness**: AI systems must be carefully monitored to avoid biases, especially when it comes to allocating resources or addressing environmental impacts across communities.
- **Energy Consumption**: While AI can help optimize energy use, training large AI models requires significant computational power, which can contribute to carbon emissions.

Despite these challenges, the future of AI in sustainability looks promising. With further advancements in AI technology, better data availability, and more collaboration between governments, businesses, and individuals, we can look forward to a greener, more sustainable future.

AI is proving to be a vital ally in the fight for a sustainable planet. From combating climate change and improving energy efficiency to conserving wildlife and enhancing food security, AI is helping us make better choices and protect our natural resources.

As we move forward, we must ensure that AI's benefits are distributed fairly, and that its use remains transparent and ethical. By harnessing AI's power for sustainability, we have the chance to create a brighter, greener future for all.

Artificial General Intelligence (AGI)

XXVIII
What is AGI?

"What if machines could think, learn, and understand the world just like humans do? What if they could adapt to any situation, solve any problem, and even create new things? That's what Artificial General Intelligence (AGI) promises."

Welcome to the exciting world of AGI, or **Artificial General Intelligence**. If you've heard the term thrown around but aren't entirely sure what it means, don't worry. We'll break it down step by step.

In today's world, when we talk about **artificial intelligence (AI)**, we're usually referring to systems that are great at doing one specific task. For example, AI can beat humans at chess, recommend songs on Spotify, or even translate languages on Google. But here's the catch: **These AI systems are narrow**—they can only do what they were specifically designed for.

Now, imagine a **machine that can do almost anything a human can do**—a machine that can learn new things, solve complex problems, understand emotions, and even come up with creative ideas. This is the essence of **AGI**. It's **not limited to a specific task**; it's **versatile**, just like us!

Defining Artificial General Intelligence (AGI)

At its core, AGI is **the next frontier in artificial intelligence**. It's a type of AI that doesn't just excel at one thing but is capable of **performing any cognitive task** that a human being can do.

Think of it this way: If you were to ask a narrow AI like Siri to help you with something beyond its capabilities, it would struggle or fail entirely. However, an AGI system could adapt and **learn on the spot**—just like how a person might pick up a new skill or knowledge and apply it to solve a problem.

To make this clearer:

- **Narrow AI**: This is the kind of AI we see today. It's trained for a specific purpose like playing a game or recognizing pictures. It can't do anything outside of its predefined task.
- **AGI**: This is a highly flexible and intelligent system that can perform any cognitive task a human can, such as thinking critically, solving novel problems, and even applying knowledge from one field to another.

Why AGI Matters

So, why should we care about AGI? After all, we've got AI systems that work pretty well, right? Well, the key difference with AGI is that **it could revolutionize everything**.

The Potential Impact on Industries:

Imagine having a **single system** that can understand and **transform every industry**—from healthcare to finance, education to entertainment. With AGI, we could:

- **Develop new medical treatments** by quickly analyzing vast amounts of data and making breakthroughs faster than human doctors could.
- **Improve efficiency in business** by automating complex decision-making and operations across various sectors.
- **Innovate in education** by personalizing learning experiences for students and providing custom-tailored content for everyone.

Everyday Life:

AGI could even change **how we live our daily lives.** Imagine a personal assistant that can organize your entire day, help you with creative projects, and even make big decisions for you—one that **truly understands your**

preferences and evolves with your needs.

The possibilities of AGI are vast. Whether it's **solving world hunger**, **tackling climate change**, or providing **personalized healthcare**, AGI could be the key to unlocking solutions that were previously unimaginable.

The Dream of AGI

Let's take a step back for a moment. **Where did the idea of AGI come from?** How did we get from the idea of intelligent machines in science fiction to what we're seeing in the world today?

From Science Fiction to Reality:

The dream of creating machines that think like humans is **not new**. It's been a topic in science fiction for decades. Think back to movies like **2001: A Space Odyssey**, where the sentient computer HAL 9000 interacted with humans, or the novel **I, Robot**, where robots were capable of learning and making decisions.

While those were fictional stories, they were grounded in a vision of intelligent machines capable of doing far more than just performing simple tasks. As **AI research has advanced**, we've moved closer to making this vision a reality. Technologies like **machine learning, deep learning**, and **neural networks** are the building blocks that have helped us get to this point.

The Shift Towards AGI:

In the past, AI was focused on **narrow tasks**. Today, we are moving toward AGI by trying to create systems that don't just perform tasks, but **understand the world** in a broader, more general sense. Researchers are developing algorithms that can **think, reason, and adapt**, much like the human brain does. Though we are still in the early stages of AGI development, we're making progress.

The idea is that once we create **AGI**, it could potentially **surpass human intelligence** in almost every domain, solving complex problems faster than any human brain could. It's still a long journey, but we're slowly but surely making strides toward that goal.

Wrapping It Up

In summary, **AGI is the next big leap** in artificial intelligence. Unlike current AI, which is highly specialized, AGI aims to create machines that can think, learn, and adapt like humans—performing any intellectual task that we can do. The potential of AGI is **massive**, with the ability to revolutionize industries, improve our daily lives, and solve some of the world's most pressing challenges.

As we move forward, we'll take a closer look at the technologies that could help us build AGI, the challenges involved, and how it might change the world as we know it. But for now, it's clear that **AGI is no longer just a dream**—it's an evolving reality. Are we ready for it?

XXIX

The Core Elements of AGI

Welcome back! In the previous chapter, we introduced the idea of **Artificial General Intelligence (AGI)**—the intelligent machines that can think, learn, and adapt like humans. Now, let's take a deeper look at the core elements that make AGI so special. What are the key features that AGI must have to truly become the **next leap in artificial intelligence**?

Think of this chapter as a **blueprint for AGI**. We'll explore what it means for a machine to **learn**, **solve problems**, **be creative**, and **make decisions**—just like you or me. Ready? Let's dive in!

Key Features of AGI

At the heart of **AGI** lies a few critical features that differentiate it from the narrow AI systems we see today. These are the characteristics that AGI must possess to function like the general intelligence of a human brain.

1. **Learning Ability:**
   The first thing that sets AGI apart is its **ability to learn**. Just like how humans can pick up new skills or learn from experience, AGI must be able to absorb new information and apply it to different situations. For example, a human can learn to bake a cake by reading a recipe, but if the recipe changes, we can still adapt and solve the problem. Similarly, AGI should be able to learn on its own, whether it's a new language, a

scientific concept, or a completely unfamiliar task.

2. **Problem-Solving**:
Humans don't need to know all the answers to solve problems. We use our judgment and reasoning abilities to figure things out. AGI must do the same. Whether it's a math puzzle, a complex business problem, or even a tricky social dilemma, an AGI system should be able to think through solutions and come up with answers that make sense. It shouldn't just follow rules but apply **logic and reasoning** to tackle **unfamiliar challenges**.

3. **Creativity**:
Creativity is often thought of as a **uniquely human trait**, but AGI will need it too. AGI systems must be able to create new ideas, think outside the box, and generate **innovative solutions**. Whether it's coming up with a new product design, composing music, or finding creative ways to solve a problem, AGI must be able to push the boundaries of thought.

4. **Decision-Making Across Different Fields**:
Unlike current AI systems that are great at solving specific problems in certain fields (like playing chess or recognizing images), **AGI should make decisions in a variety of contexts**. Whether it's health, business, technology, or social situations, an AGI system should be capable of making sound decisions that are **contextually appropriate** and **aligned with human values**.

Adaptability: The Human-Like Edge

Let's get into something that's really special about AGI: **Adaptability**.
One of the biggest challenges in building AGI is making sure that it can **adapt** to **new and unpredictable situations**—just like humans do. Think about this: as a human, if you're faced with a new challenge, you don't need to have a manual or specific instructions to know how to solve it. You **apply your past experiences**, **use your intuition**, and **figure it out**.

For example, let's say you've never used a new phone before. You might have no idea where the settings are, but you can still **learn how to navigate the phone** and figure it out within a few minutes. AGI needs to do this too. It should be able to **understand unfamiliar tasks** and **find solutions** without requiring someone to program it for every new problem.

This **learning-on-the-go** feature will be a key part of what makes AGI feel **human-like**. Imagine a machine that doesn't just perform specific tasks but can **learn**, adapt, and grow in real-time. This adaptability is what will **set AGI apart from any AI system we've seen** so far.

Cognitive Flexibility and Common Sense

Let's break this down: when we talk about **cognitive flexibility**, we're talking about how easily an intelligence can **switch between tasks, apply knowledge from one area to another**, and **adjust to new situations**. Imagine being able to switch from fixing your car to writing a poem to solving a business problem—all without breaking a sweat. Humans are naturally **cognitively flexible**, and it's one of the reasons why we're able to succeed in so many different fields.

For AGI to truly be **general** and **intelligent**, it will need this same kind of flexibility. Here's why:

- **Task Switching**: An AGI system should be able to **switch between various tasks** as seamlessly as humans do. Whether it's cooking dinner, solving a coding problem, or negotiating a contract, it should be able to handle different tasks and switch its approach based on what's needed.
- **Applying Knowledge to New Contexts**: Right now, AI systems struggle to transfer knowledge from one area to another. For example, an AI trained to play chess might know everything about chess, but it's **useless** when it comes to anything else. AGI, on the other hand, should be able to **apply the knowledge it's learned** to **solve new problems** in completely different areas—this is cognitive flexibility in action.

Now, think about **common sense**. Humans don't need to learn **every single detail** about how the world works. We have **intuitive knowledge**—like knowing that if we spill a drink on the floor, it will make the surface wet. This **common sense** helps us navigate the world effectively. AGI must be equipped with this kind of **general knowledge**. It should understand basic principles about the world, even if it doesn't have specific data for a situation.

For example, if an AGI is tasked with making a decision about whether a robot should walk into a room with a cup of water, it should **understand the risk** of spilling that water and adjust its actions accordingly. This is the kind of **practical knowledge** that makes a system behave **intelligently**—without needing a complete manual for every action.

Wrapping It Up

In this chapter, we've looked at the **core elements** that AGI needs to function like a human-level intelligence. We talked about the **key features of AGI**, including **learning ability**, **problem-solving**, **creativity**, and **decision-making**. Then, we explored **adaptability**—AGI's ability to learn and adjust on the fly, much like humans do. Finally, we discussed **cognitive flexibility** and **common sense**, which are essential for AGI to perform a wide variety of tasks and understand the world in a way that feels intuitive.

In the next chapter, we'll dive deeper into **the technology that's helping AGI come to life**. We'll take a closer look at the **neural networks**, **machine learning models**, and **algorithms** that are the foundation of AGI systems. So, stay tuned—AGI is getting closer to reality, and we're just getting started!

XXX
AGI vs. Narrow AI: What's the Difference?

Alright, now that we've covered what **AGI** is and what it should be able to do, it's time to take a step back and look at how **AGI** compares to the **AI systems** we encounter today. These systems are often referred to as **Narrow AI**—but why is that the case? And how will **AGI** be different?

In this chapter, we'll explore the world of **Narrow AI** and explain how it's useful for specific tasks, but also why we need AGI to take the next step. Think of Narrow AI as an expert in one area, and AGI as a jack-of-all-trades, capable of doing **almost anything**. Let's break this down.

Narrow AI Explained

So, what exactly is **Narrow AI**? To put it simply, Narrow AI is any artificial intelligence that is **designed** to perform a **specific task** or set of tasks. It's really good at what it does, but it doesn't know how to do much else. Imagine a **specialized tool**—it works incredibly well for one job, but it's useless outside of that job.

Here are a few examples of Narrow AI that you've probably encountered:

1. **Language Translation:**
   Think about Google Translate or other translation apps. These tools use Narrow AI to translate text from one language to another. They're **great at** translating **common phrases** and **text** in real-time, but they don't

understand the **cultural context** or **nuances** of the language. If you asked it to translate a poem or a joke, it might not do so accurately. It's doing a very specific job, but it can't think outside that task.

2. **Image Recognition**:

Have you used facial recognition on your phone or social media platforms? That's another example of Narrow AI. It can **identify faces** in pictures, and **tag people** automatically, but it doesn't understand who those people are, their relationships, or why they might be in that photo. It's limited to recognizing patterns, like shapes and faces, but it doesn't truly "understand" what it sees.

3. **Playing Chess**:

AI systems like **Deep Blue** (which beat the world chess champion in the 1990s) or more modern ones like **AlphaZero** are masters of chess. They can calculate moves, predict outcomes, and make strategic decisions that humans can't match. But here's the catch: they're **great at chess**—nothing else. If you ask them to play checkers or solve a math problem, they'll be **completely lost**. They are **narrowly specialized**.

So, what makes these systems "narrow"? **They're specialized in one specific task** and excel at it, but they **can't transfer** their knowledge to different tasks. They have no ability to **learn beyond their set tasks**, which is why they're labeled "Narrow" AI.

The Leap to General Intelligence

Now, imagine a system that isn't limited to just one task, like those examples we just discussed. This is where **Artificial General Intelligence (AGI)** comes into play. AGI goes **beyond** the single-task, one-dimensional focus of Narrow AI.

Let's break it down:

AGI isn't just a **specialized expert** in one field. It's a **multitasker** that can perform a **wide range of tasks**, **learn new things on its own**, and **apply knowledge across different areas**. While Narrow AI works within the constraints of a defined task, AGI can **think, adapt**, and **solve new, unfamiliar problems**—just like humans do.

Here's an example to help you picture the difference:

- A Narrow AI system trained to **diagnose diseases** from medical images is fantastic at spotting signs of **pneumonia** in chest X-rays. However, it's not going to help much if you suddenly need it to **design a marketing campaign** or **write a song**.
- But, an AGI system could look at **the health data**, **diagnose the disease**, **suggest treatments**, and then, if needed, **switch to creative tasks** like writing a report, building a team strategy, or even coming up with a brand-new way to approach a public health crisis. It would be able to **switch between tasks seamlessly**—not just follow preset rules or formulas.

AGI will be able to **connect the dots** between different domains of knowledge, understanding the **context** and **relationships** between them, and making decisions that take everything into account.

Real-World Examples of Narrow AI and the Need for AGI

So why do we still need AGI if Narrow AI is so useful? Let's explore why AGI is the next big thing, and why it's needed in areas where today's AI just can't keep up.

1. **In Healthcare**:
   Narrow AI can **analyze medical images** and **diagnose diseases** based on patterns. But it can't **explain** the disease, **propose treatment plans**, or **consider a patient's entire medical history**. AGI, however, could **analyze the entire medical picture**, from images to patient records, and **make decisions** about how to treat the patient—based on multiple factors like lifestyle, environment, and genetics. It could even **suggest new treatments** or **innovate solutions** to problems that Narrow AI couldn't predict.
2. **In Business**:
   Companies today use Narrow AI to **automate customer service**, **recommend products**, and even **analyze data** to find patterns in sales. But these tools are limited—they **can't think strategically**. AGI, on the other hand, could **generate new business models**, **analyze market trends**, and **predict future shifts**. It would help leaders **make smarter decisions** by considering not just data, but also **external factors** like geopolitical events, consumer behavior, and global economics.

3. **In Creativity**:
   Narrow AI is starting to make waves in the creative world, too. It can **generate art**, **compose music**, and **write scripts**. But these creations are based on existing styles, templates, and rules—Narrow AI doesn't actually "create" in the same way humans do. AGI could **push the boundaries of creativity**, coming up with entirely **new genres**, **innovative ideas**, and **original artistic expressions** that we couldn't even imagine.

Wrapping It Up

In this chapter, we've learned that **Narrow AI** is great at specific tasks, but it lacks the ability to go beyond those tasks. **AGI**, on the other hand, is the ultimate multitasker—able to learn, adapt, and solve problems across a wide range of fields, just like humans.

While today's AI systems help in **specific areas** like language translation, image recognition, and healthcare, **AGI** will unlock a new era of **intelligent machines** that can do so much more. AGI will enable us to solve **complex problems**, create **innovative solutions**, and understand the world in ways that narrow systems can't.

As we move toward building AGI, we need to understand the **limits of Narrow AI** and why **AGI** is crucial for handling the **multifaceted challenges** of tomorrow. The leap from Narrow AI to AGI represents the next major milestone in artificial intelligence, and we're just getting started!

XXXI

The Building Blocks of AGI

In this chapter, we're going to dive into the **essential components** that will make AGI possible. Building an **Artificial General Intelligence** (AGI) is like constructing a very sophisticated machine that doesn't just follow a set of rules. It needs to **think, learn,** and **adapt** on its own—much like a human. But how do we build something that can do that?

The answer lies in a combination of powerful technologies that already exist today but are being pushed to their limits to make AGI a reality. To help you understand, think of these building blocks as **the tools** or **ingredients** needed to bake a cake—each one plays a crucial role in creating a truly intelligent system.

Let's break down the main building blocks of AGI in simple terms.

The Role of Machine Learning and Neural Networks

When we think about **AGI**, one of the most important ingredients is **machine learning**. But what is machine learning, and why is it so important for AGI?

Imagine you're teaching a child how to recognize animals. You start by showing them pictures of a dog, a cat, a lion, and so on. Over time, the child starts to **learn** the differences between them. They get better at identifying animals because they've seen many examples and practiced recognizing key features, like a dog's ears or a lion's mane.

Machine learning works in a similar way. It's a type of technology that allows computers to **learn from data** instead of being explicitly programmed. For instance, a machine learning model can be trained to recognize cats in photos by being shown thousands of cat images and learning patterns from those examples.

But here's where it gets more exciting: **Neural networks** are a type of machine learning system inspired by the human brain. They are made up of layers of artificial "neurons" that work together to process and learn from data. These networks are designed to **mimic** how our brain works—passing information from one layer to another, just like how our brain processes signals between neurons.

In AGI, these **neural networks** will help the system **think, learn, and reason**. For example, an AGI system could use neural networks to **analyze data**, make **decisions**, and **improve over time** by learning from experience—just like how we humans get better at tasks as we practice them.

Reinforcement Learning and Self-Improvement

One of the most exciting aspects of AGI is its ability to **learn from experience** and **improve itself**. This concept is at the heart of something called **reinforcement learning**. But what does that mean?

Imagine you're teaching a dog to fetch a ball. The dog tries, sometimes it gets the ball, sometimes it doesn't. When it gets it right, you reward the dog with a treat, reinforcing the good behavior. Over time, the dog learns that fetching the ball results in a treat, so it's more likely to do it again.

This is how **reinforcement learning** works in AI. The AI tries something, gets feedback (a reward or a punishment), and then **adjusts** its behavior based on that feedback. This **feedback loop** helps the AI improve and get better over time.

Now, for AGI, this kind of learning is critical. It's not just about following instructions; it's about **adapting** and **improving** based on the environment and experiences. The more an AGI system experiences, the better it can handle new and unexpected situations.

For instance, let's say we have an AGI system that is learning to **drive a car**. It would start by making decisions based on a set of rules, but over time, it would **learn from its experiences** on the road, such as how to navigate complex traffic situations, how to react to unusual events (like a child running into the street), and how to make better decisions with more information.

The ultimate goal of **reinforcement learning** in AGI is to create a system that can **self-improve**—just like how we humans get better at something through **trial and error**.

Multimodal Learning

AGI won't just be great at one thing. To be truly **general intelligence**, it needs to understand and process different types of information—just like humans do. For example, humans use **sight, sound, touch**, and even **taste** to understand the world around them. AGI needs to do something similar.

This is where **multimodal learning** comes in. In simple terms, multimodal learning means that an AGI system can **combine and understand multiple forms of information**. It's not just about reading text or hearing sounds separately; it's about integrating and understanding the **relationships** between them all.

Let's use an example: Suppose you ask an AGI system to describe a **scene**. If it only knows how to process **images**, it might identify an object as a "tree" but won't know anything about **why** the tree is important in the scene. However, with multimodal learning, an AGI system can **combine** text, images, and even sound to create a deeper understanding of the situation. It might know that the tree is in a park, it's autumn, and there's a wind rustling through its leaves.

This ability to **cross-reference information** from **different sources** makes AGI incredibly powerful. It will be able to **learn about the world** in a way that's more **human-like**, understanding how different pieces of information connect and work together. This is a huge leap from Narrow AI, which typically processes only one type of data at a time, like just text or just images.

Wrapping It Up

So, what have we learned in this chapter?

1. **Machine Learning and Neural Networks**:
   These are the building blocks that will allow AGI to think, learn, and reason. Just like the human brain, AGI systems will rely on layers of

artificial neurons to process information and get smarter over time.

2. **Reinforcement Learning**:

    AGI needs to be able to **learn from experience** and improve, just like we do. Reinforcement learning enables AGI systems to **adapt** and become better at tasks through trial and error.

3. **Multimodal Learning**:

    AGI will need to understand information from multiple sources (images, text, sound, etc.) and be able to combine these to make smarter decisions, much like how humans use all their senses to understand the world.

XXXII

Can Generative AI Lead to AGI?

In this chapter, we're going to explore an exciting question: **Can Generative AI lead us to AGI?** It's an important question because the advancements in **Generative AI** are giving us a glimpse of what's possible, and people are wondering—could this be the key to creating **Artificial General Intelligence (AGI)**?

Let's dive in and break it all down.

What Generative AI Brings to the Table

You may have heard of **Generative AI** tools like **GPT-3** (a language model), **DALL·E** (which creates images from text prompts), or other similar systems. These models are **incredibly powerful**, and they are already performing tasks that were once thought to be exclusive to human creativity, such as writing stories, making artwork, and solving problems. So, how do these tools contribute to AGI?

Think of **Generative AI** as a supercharged **creative assistant**. It can write essays, generate music, design images, and even help with technical tasks like coding—all from scratch. These models learn from vast amounts of data (texts, images, etc.) and generate something new based on that knowledge.

Here's the magic: **Generative AI** doesn't just **repeat** information it has seen before; it **creates new things**—whether that's text, images, or even solutions to complex problems. This ability to **generate original content** is a huge step towards AGI. Why? Because it shows us that machines can go beyond simply answering questions or following instructions. They can **create**, which is a trait closely associated with human intelligence.

Why Creativity and Flexibility Matter for AGI

Now, let's talk about **creativity** and **flexibility**. These are two key traits that are essential for AGI to evolve and truly function like a human brain.

1. **Creativity**:
   When you think about humans, one of the things that set us apart is our **ability to think creatively**. We can come up with new ideas, imagine things that don't exist, and make connections between completely different concepts. For example, an artist might combine elements from nature and technology to create a futuristic painting. Or a writer might mix a love story with elements of mystery or fantasy.

   Generative AI systems like GPT-3 and DALL·E are beginning to show these **creative abilities**. GPT-3 can write stories in any genre, create poetry, or even make jokes. DALL·E can generate **artwork** from simple text prompts, like "a futuristic city at sunset" or "a cat wearing a suit." The creativity of these models suggests that **machines** can learn to **think outside the box**—just like humans do.

   So, why does creativity matter for AGI? Because **creating new ideas and solving problems in novel ways** is a hallmark of general intelligence. To achieve AGI, a system needs to be able to do more than just process information—it needs to **generate new possibilities** and think creatively in various situations, just like humans.

1. **Flexibility**:
   Another key trait for AGI is **flexibility**—the ability to **adapt** to a wide range of tasks and environments. We humans can learn a lot of different skills—be it painting, solving math problems, or learning a new language—and apply that knowledge across multiple areas. For example, a person who can write fiction might also be able to write a technical report or analyze a business situation.

Generative AI is showing early signs of flexibility. It can generate **text** in multiple styles, create images in different genres, and even write code. It's **not confined** to just one task but can **adapt** to many different needs. This flexibility is one of the building blocks needed for AGI, as it shows that a machine can handle **varied tasks** with ease.

Bridging the Gap

So far, we've seen that **Generative AI** is showing incredible progress in areas like creativity and flexibility. But, here's the big question: **Can this lead to AGI?**

The answer is **not quite yet**, but we're on the right path. **Generative AI** models are certainly advancing, but there are still important gaps that need to be filled before we have true **Artificial General Intelligence**. These gaps include the ability to reason deeply, **understand complex relationships**, and **think critically** across all kinds of tasks, much like how humans approach problems in daily life.

In other words, while **Generative AI** is impressive, it's still a **specialized system**. It can be amazing at tasks like writing a novel, creating art, or answering questions, but it's not yet able to handle the full range of cognitive functions that AGI requires.

Here's an analogy: **Generative AI** is like a highly skilled **artist**. It can paint, draw, and even invent new artistic styles. But AGI, on the other hand, would be like an artist who can also **solve mathematical problems**, **plan a business strategy**, and **learn how to play the violin**—all with equal skill and flexibility.

The road from Generative AI to **AGI** involves adding even **more depth** and **versatility**. AGI needs to understand not just **what** something is, but **why** it's important, how it connects with other pieces of knowledge, and how to apply that knowledge in novel situations.

Wrapping It Up

Let's summarize the key takeaways from this chapter:

1. **Generative AI's Role**:
   Models like GPT-3 and DALL·E show incredible creativity and flexibility. They can generate original content, solve problems, and adapt to various

tasks—important steps toward AGI.

2. **Creativity and Flexibility**:
These qualities are essential for AGI. **Creativity** allows systems to generate new ideas, while **flexibility** enables them to apply knowledge in diverse contexts.

3. **Bridging the Gap**:
While Generative AI has come a long way, we're still not there yet. AGI requires even more **advanced reasoning**, **understanding**, and **application** of knowledge across multiple areas. Generative AI is an important piece of the puzzle, but there's still a journey ahead.

XXXIII

The Future of AGI: What Lies Ahead?

Welcome to a fascinating chapter about the future of **Artificial General Intelligence (AGI)**! We've explored what AGI is, how it's different from narrow AI, and how **Generative AI** is paving the way for its development. But now, let's look ahead and ask: **What's next for AGI?**

The future of AGI is a mix of excitement, mystery, and sometimes uncertainty. Let's talk about what experts predict for AGI's development, the role of **open-source** initiatives in shaping AGI, and whether we can even fully imagine what AGI might do in the future.

Predictions for AGI Development

The big question is: **When will AGI arrive?** While no one can say for sure, experts have some **predictions** about when we might start seeing AGI and how it will change our lives. Some say it could happen within the next **20-50 years**, while others believe it might take longer. The truth is, predicting the future of AGI is a bit like predicting the weather—it's a mix of science, observation, and a little bit of guesswork.

However, there's no doubt that **AGI will revolutionize** nearly every part of our lives. Imagine a world where you have a personal assistant that doesn't just answer your questions, but can also **solve complex problems**, **innovate**, and even **create** new solutions in ways we haven't thought of yet. This could mean significant changes in fields like medicine, education, entertainment, and even governance.

- **Medicine**: AGI might help doctors **diagnose diseases** more accurately or come up with new treatments faster than ever before.
- **Education**: AGI could provide **personalized learning experiences**, adapting to each student's needs and learning pace.
- **Business and Finance**: AGI could analyze **massive amounts of data** to predict trends, make decisions, and guide companies to more success.

But **AGI's impact** won't just be about making tasks more efficient. It could lead to a complete **transformation** of how we think about work, creativity, and even our **relationships with technology**.

However, there are also risks involved. Will AGI be used responsibly? Could it disrupt job markets? These are questions that researchers, businesses, and policymakers will have to grapple with as AGI begins to develop.

The Role of Open-Source AGI

Now, here's an interesting twist: **open-source** projects are playing a huge role in shaping the future of AGI. You might be familiar with the concept of **open-source software**—it's software that is freely available for anyone to use, modify, and share. Well, this same idea is starting to apply to **AGI development**.

But why does this matter? Let's think about it:

1. **Collaboration and Transparency**:
   Open-source projects allow people from all over the world to **collaborate** on AGI research and development. This means that no single company or country controls AGI, which can make the development process **more transparent** and **ethical**.
2. **Innovation**:
   By being **open-source**, developers can experiment, test new ideas, and share knowledge freely. This could lead to faster **advancements** in AGI, as everyone works together to solve complex problems and push the boundaries of what AGI can do.
3. **Ethical AGI**:
   One of the major concerns about AGI is ensuring that it's developed

ethically and used for the benefit of everyone. Open-source development helps ensure that there are **multiple checks and balances**. When many different people and organizations have a hand in shaping AGI, it becomes less likely that it will be developed in a way that's harmful or biased.

Examples of open-source AGI projects already exist, and they are growing. Communities of developers are working on creating **AGI systems** that can learn and adapt from different data sources, ultimately leading to **more inclusive** and **diverse AGI systems**.

So, the future of AGI isn't just in the hands of big tech companies—**the community**, driven by **open-source** collaboration, will play a pivotal role in shaping the future of intelligent machines.

AGI and the Limits of Human Imagination

Now, we get into the real mystery of AGI: **Can we even imagine all the things AGI will be capable of?** This is where things get interesting. When humans first imagined **artificial intelligence**, they thought of it as a tool for automating basic tasks. But over time, AI has evolved in ways that no one could have predicted—writing poetry, diagnosing diseases, and creating art. It's like **science fiction** coming to life!

So, what does this mean for **AGI**? Well, the truth is, AGI might be so advanced that it will **surpass our ability to imagine**. It could create solutions to problems we haven't even thought of yet. It might come up with innovative ideas that are so outside-the-box, we couldn't even picture them. And that's exciting, but also a little intimidating. **Will AGI be able to think in ways we can't even begin to understand?**

Think about this: The **human brain** is an incredibly complex machine, and we've only just started to understand how it works. AGI, which mimics human-like intelligence, could eventually become even **smarter** and **more capable** than we are, leading us into a future where the **impossible becomes possible**.

And here's the crazy part—**AGI could even create new forms of intelligence**, beyond human understanding. It could generate its own way of thinking, reasoning, and learning that we haven't even imagined yet.

Wrapping Up: What's Next for AGI?

To wrap up, we've learned a lot about the **future of AGI** in this chapter:

1. **AGI's Impact**: Predictions for AGI's arrival suggest that it will **revolutionize** many industries and our daily lives, with new breakthroughs in medicine, education, business, and beyond. However, its development comes with its own set of challenges and risks.
2. **Open-Source AGI**: Open-source projects are helping shape the future of AGI by allowing **global collaboration**, increasing **transparency**, and ensuring **ethical development**.
3. **The Limits of Imagination**: The full extent of AGI's capabilities might be beyond our **current imagination**. It could bring new ideas, new solutions, and even new forms of intelligence that we haven't thought of yet.

In the coming years, AGI will continue to evolve, and while we can't predict everything about its future, one thing is for sure: **The possibilities are endless**. As we stand on the brink of AGI's potential, the world as we know it may change in ways we can't even begin to understand. But that's the exciting part—it's a journey that will challenge our imaginations and push the boundaries of human potential.

Stay tuned, because the future of AGI is just beginning!

Robots, AI Agents, and Chatbots: The Intersection of AI and Human Interaction

XXXIV

What Are Robots, AI Agents, and Chatbots?

Understanding the Difference: Robots, AI Agents, and Chatbots

Let's start by clearing up the terms that are often thrown around in conversations about AI—**robots**, **AI agents**, and **chatbots**. At first glance, they might seem similar, but each plays a different role in the world of artificial intelligence.

1. **Robots** are physical machines designed to perform specific tasks. Think of them as the "hands" and "legs" of artificial intelligence. Robots can range from simple machines that move parts on an assembly line to complex machines like **autonomous delivery robots** or **surgical robots** that perform medical procedures.

2. **AI Agents**, on the other hand, are software-based systems designed to carry out tasks or make decisions without needing human intervention. They are like digital brains that can think and make decisions. These AI agents could be in the form of virtual assistants like **Siri** or **Alexa**, or even autonomous systems that control self-driving cars. AI agents don't necessarily have a physical body; they work behind the scenes, performing tasks and solving problems.

3. **Chatbots** are a special type of AI agent that can communicate with people through text or voice. When you visit a website or use customer support, you've probably encountered a **chatbot**. It's a program that can understand what you're typing and respond in a way that mimics human conversation. Chatbots can handle tasks like answering questions, providing information, or even solving simple problems. **Customer service chatbots** are a good example of this.

The Evolution of AI in Human Interaction

Now, let's take a step back and look at how these technologies evolved over time. In the beginning, AI was quite simple. Early AI systems were **rule-based**, which means they followed a set of instructions that humans programmed into them. For example, early chatbots could only respond with preset answers to certain questions, but they couldn't handle anything unexpected.

Over the years, things started changing. With the advent of more **advanced machine learning** and **natural language processing** techniques, AI systems began to learn from the data they were given. They didn't just follow pre-programmed rules—they began to **adapt** and **improvise**. This allowed them to become much smarter and more flexible.

In the past decade, the rise of **deep learning** has made AI systems even more capable. Now, robots, AI agents, and chatbots can learn and solve problems in ways that were previously only possible for humans. For instance, a **chatbot** now doesn't just respond to specific commands, but can actually understand the **context** of what you're saying, which allows it to engage in more meaningful conversations.

Similarly, **robots** today are no longer just machines doing repetitive tasks. They can **sense** their surroundings, make decisions in real time, and even **learn** new tasks. In fact, in industries like healthcare, **robotic surgery** is becoming a reality, where robots assist doctors with precision and accuracy.

And what about **AI agents**? These are the virtual assistants on our smartphones, computers, or smart speakers. Over time, they've gone from answering simple questions like "What's the weather?" to helping us plan our day, manage tasks, and even make decisions based on personal preferences.

Everyday Examples of Robots, AI Agents, and Chatbots

So, how do we interact with these technologies in our daily lives? Let's look at a few examples:

- **Siri and Alexa**: These are great examples of AI agents that we use almost every day. They can perform a variety of tasks like setting reminders, answering questions, playing music, and even controlling smart home devices. They make life easier by handling basic tasks that would otherwise take up our time.
- **Autonomous Delivery Robots**: Have you ever seen those small, robot-like vehicles moving around city streets, delivering food or packages? These are robots powered by AI agents. They navigate streets, avoid obstacles, and deliver goods autonomously, often without any human intervention.
- **Customer Service Chatbots**: Many companies now use **chatbots** on their websites or apps to handle customer service inquiries. If you've ever needed help while shopping online or tracking a package, you've probably interacted with a chatbot. It might have been a simple question like "Where is my order?" or something more complex like troubleshooting an issue with a product. Chatbots are designed to understand your questions and provide relevant answers instantly.
- **Robot Vacuums**: Another everyday example of robots at work is the **robot vacuum**, like the **Roomba**. These robots are designed to autonomously clean your home, navigating around furniture, detecting dirt, and even returning to their charging station when the task is done. They are powered by AI agents that allow them to make decisions about how and when to clean.

These examples show how AI, robots, and chatbots are becoming integrated into our daily routines, helping us with tasks, improving convenience, and even offering new possibilities for how we interact with technology. Whether it's asking a question, ordering a meal, or having a robot vacuum your house, these AI-powered technologies are all around us.

XXXV

The Rise of AI Agents: What They Are and How They Work

What Is an AI Agent?

Let's imagine for a moment that you have a personal assistant—one who can do more than just answer your questions or set reminders. This assistant can **think**, **learn**, and **adapt** to new situations without you having to give it step-by-step instructions. This is what we mean when we talk about an **AI agent**.

An **AI agent** is essentially a computer system designed to perform specific tasks autonomously, with little or no human intervention. Unlike basic programs that follow pre-defined rules, AI agents are capable of making decisions, learning from experiences, and adapting to new situations, much like a human would. The goal is for these agents to take over certain tasks that humans do, but with a level of efficiency and accuracy that can improve over time.

To put it simply: Think of AI agents as smart, self-learning assistants who don't need constant guidance. They can handle a variety of tasks—whether it's organizing your schedule, driving your car, or securing your home—without much help from you.

The Core Technologies Behind AI Agents

Now that we know what an AI agent is, let's dive into how they work. These smart systems are powered by a combination of technologies that allow them to think, learn, and make decisions. Let's break down some of the core technologies behind AI agents:

1. **Reinforcement Learning**: This is one of the key technologies that allows AI agents to learn and improve over time. In simple terms, reinforcement learning is like teaching a dog new tricks by giving it rewards when it does something right. For example, an AI agent might start by performing a task randomly. If it does something that leads to a good outcome, it gets a "reward" (a positive result or feedback). Over time, it learns which actions lead to better results, just like a dog learns which tricks earn treats.

2. **Natural Language Processing (NLP)**: Have you ever spoken to Siri or Alexa and asked them to play a song or give you the weather forecast? That's **NLP** at work. NLP allows AI agents to understand human language, interpret meaning, and respond in a way that feels natural. It helps AI agents interpret the words you use, figure out the context, and generate appropriate responses. This makes communication with AI agents feel more like interacting with a human, rather than typing commands into a machine.

3. **Computer Vision**: Computer vision is the ability of an AI agent to "see" and understand visual information from the world around it. This technology allows AI agents to analyze images or video, identify objects, and make sense of what's happening in their environment. For example, self-driving cars use computer vision to recognize pedestrians, traffic signs, and other vehicles, which helps them navigate the roads safely.

These technologies combine to enable AI agents to think, learn, and interact with the world in ways that we traditionally only expected from humans.

Real-world Examples of AI Agents

AI agents are no longer a concept from science fiction. They are actively shaping our world in many ways, with applications in everyday life. Let's look at some real-world examples of AI agents:

1. **Virtual Assistants (Siri, Alexa, Google Assistant)**: If you've ever asked your phone or smart speaker to play music, answer a question, or set a reminder, you've interacted with an AI agent. These virtual assistants are powered by natural language processing and machine learning. They learn from your voice commands and adjust their responses over time to become more accurate and efficient. For example, Siri learns your preferences for certain apps, music genres, or even how you phrase things, making it more helpful the more you use it.

2. **Self-Driving Cars**: One of the most exciting and futuristic examples of AI agents is the **self-driving car**. Powered by AI agents that use sensors, cameras, and machine learning algorithms, these cars can navigate the roads, avoid obstacles, and make driving decisions without human intervention. They process huge amounts of data in real time, allowing them to learn and improve their driving skills as they encounter different driving conditions.

3. **AI-Powered Security Systems**: Many modern security systems use AI agents to monitor properties, detect intruders, and even recognize faces. These systems use **computer vision** to scan for unusual activity and notify homeowners or authorities about potential security breaches. Unlike traditional systems that might simply trigger an alarm when motion is detected, AI-powered security systems can intelligently assess situations and make decisions based on what they see.

4. **AI in Healthcare**: AI agents are also transforming the healthcare industry. For example, AI systems can help doctors make better decisions by analyzing medical data, detecting patterns, and suggesting potential diagnoses. These AI agents don't replace doctors—they act as tools that assist in diagnosing illnesses or managing treatment plans by offering recommendations based on vast amounts of medical information.

5. **Customer Service Chatbots**: If you've interacted with a customer service chatbot, you've encountered another type of AI agent. These chatbots can understand your inquiries, provide solutions, and even carry on a conversation in a way that feels natural. They are powered by natural language processing and machine learning, meaning they can get smarter with each interaction.

Why Are AI Agents Important?

AI agents are not just cool gadgets or futuristic technology. They represent a fundamental shift in how we interact with machines and solve problems. They're already making tasks more efficient, reducing human error, and opening up possibilities for new solutions that were once unimaginable.

Whether it's automating everyday chores, improving decision-making, or even enhancing healthcare, AI agents are here to stay—and they're only going to get smarter and more capable in the future.

In this chapter, we've learned that AI agents are intelligent systems that can perform tasks autonomously, powered by technologies like machine learning, natural language processing, and computer vision. From virtual assistants to self-driving cars, AI agents are already becoming part of our daily lives, changing the way we interact with the world and opening up new possibilities for the future.

XXXVI
Chatbots and Conversational AI: Revolutionizing Customer Interaction

What Are Chatbots and How Do They Work?

Imagine you're trying to solve an issue with your internet provider, but it's 2 a.m., and their support team is offline. Enter the **chatbot**—an AI-powered system that can chat with you and help resolve your issue, even when human agents are unavailable. Chatbots are digital assistants designed to simulate human conversation and help with a variety of tasks. They are used everywhere, from helping you book tickets to assisting with customer service, and even providing entertainment or health advice.

Think of a chatbot as your virtual helper—an intelligent system that answers your questions, performs actions, and helps you solve problems without needing a human on the other end. When you visit a website and a message pops up saying, "How can I help you today?" that's usually a chatbot, ready to assist.

But how do these digital helpers actually work? Chatbots interact with you by using **text or voice input**, understanding your questions, and then generating responses. These responses may be pre-programmed (for simple tasks) or generated on the fly (using advanced AI techniques). The core idea is to make the interaction as natural as possible, so it feels like you're chatting with a human, not a machine.

Chatbot Technologies: NLP and Deep Learning

So, how does a chatbot understand and respond to your questions like a real person would? The magic lies in two powerful technologies: **Natural Language Processing (NLP)** and **deep learning**.

1. **Natural Language Processing (NLP)**: NLP is a field of AI that focuses on enabling machines to understand and interact using human language. Just like when you speak to a friend, you use sentences, tone, and context to convey meaning. NLP helps chatbots "understand" those same nuances in your words, allowing them to make sense of what you're asking and respond appropriately. It's what enables a chatbot to decipher everything from simple commands like "What's the weather today?" to more complex queries like, "Can you help me track my order?"

In essence, NLP acts as the bridge between human communication and machines, turning what you say into something the computer can understand and act upon.

1. **Deep Learning**: Deep learning is another crucial piece of the puzzle. It involves training chatbots to recognize patterns in vast amounts of data—like a massive library of conversations. The more data the chatbot processes, the better it gets at predicting what the user might want and responding accurately. It's similar to how you might learn a language by listening to native speakers—over time, you start understanding the flow of conversations and respond appropriately. Deep learning helps chatbots improve their responses and adapt to new topics or ways of speaking.

By combining these technologies, chatbots can "learn" from every interaction and provide more intelligent, context-aware responses over time.

Real-World Applications of Chatbots

You've probably already interacted with chatbots without even realizing it. These little virtual assistants are everywhere and are transforming the way companies do business. Let's take a look at some of the key areas where chatbots are making a big difference:

1. **Customer Support**: One of the most popular uses for chatbots is **customer service**. Imagine you're having trouble with your online order. Instead of calling customer support and waiting for hours, you can simply chat with a bot on the company's website. The chatbot can instantly provide answers, resolve issues, or escalate the matter to a human agent if needed. Many companies use chatbots to handle routine inquiries—like checking the status of an order, answering product questions, or providing help with a service—so that human agents can focus on more complex problems.

2. **Lead Generation**: Chatbots aren't just there to solve problems—they can help companies attract new customers too. For instance, if you visit a website and a chatbot pops up offering to help you learn more about their product, that's a chatbot driving **lead generation**. It can ask questions to qualify you as a potential customer and even schedule a meeting with a salesperson. This means businesses can engage with potential clients 24/7, without needing a human staff member to be present.

3. **24/7 Service**: One of the biggest advantages of chatbots is that they don't sleep! They can provide assistance around the clock, whether it's late at night or during holidays when customer service teams might be unavailable. This constant availability means companies can ensure they never leave their customers without help.

4. **E-commerce**: Chatbots are also changing how we shop online. Many e-commerce platforms now use chatbots to recommend products, answer questions about size or availability, and even help with payments. Imagine asking a chatbot, "I need a new pair of sneakers," and it instantly provides you with a list of options based on your style preferences. This makes shopping quicker and more personalized.

Conversational AI and the Future of Human Interaction

Chatbots are great, but **conversational AI** takes things to the next level. Conversational AI is a term used to describe AI systems that can engage in more complex, dynamic, and natural conversations with humans. While traditional chatbots are often limited to answering simple questions, conversational AI systems can hold deeper, more meaningful dialogues.

For example, imagine chatting with an AI agent who not only responds to your direct requests but also understands the context and nuances of what you say. If you ask about the weather and follow up with a question about nearby restaurants, the AI would remember your earlier question and provide relevant suggestions. This level of understanding allows conversational AI to make interactions feel more **human-like**.

Conversational AI systems are also starting to gain **emotional intelligence**, allowing them to gauge your tone, recognize frustration, and adjust responses accordingly. For instance, if you're upset about a service issue, a conversational AI might respond in a more empathetic way, trying to calm you down or offer solutions faster.

In the future, we may see conversational AI being used in **therapy**, **education**, or **personal coaching**—helping people work through emotional issues, learn new skills, or get advice on a variety of topics.

Why Are Chatbots and Conversational AI Important?

Chatbots and conversational AI are revolutionizing the way businesses interact with customers. They save time, reduce operational costs, and provide faster, more efficient service. But beyond that, they're **enhancing user experience**, making it easier for people to get help, solve problems, and engage with brands on their terms.

As AI continues to improve, chatbots will become even smarter, more intuitive, and more personalized. What was once a simple tool for answering basic questions will evolve into a fully integrated, 24/7 assistant capable of handling almost any interaction—across industries and platforms.

XXXVII

Robots in Industry: Automation in Action

What Role Do Robots Play in Industry?

Have you ever wondered how a car gets built in just a few hours, or how warehouses can ship thousands of packages every day without human hands touching them? The answer often lies in **robots**. These machines are not just a part of science fiction anymore; they're changing the way industries work, from **manufacturing** to **agriculture** and even **healthcare**.

Let's start with the **manufacturing industry**. In car factories, for example, robots are used to weld parts together, paint cars, and assemble components with incredible precision and speed. These robots don't get tired, and they can work non-stop, allowing factories to produce more products in less time and with fewer errors.

In **logistics**, robots are speeding up the process of sorting and delivering packages. For example, in warehouses, robots can move products around, scan barcodes, and prepare orders for shipment—all without needing a break. This not only increases productivity but also improves accuracy and efficiency.

But it's not just about physical labor. **Healthcare** is also seeing a rise in robotic technology. Surgeons can now use robotic arms for precise surgeries, and robots can help with tasks like delivering medication or assisting elderly patients with mobility. Similarly, **agriculture** is benefiting from robots that plant crops, harvest fruits, and monitor soil conditions, making farming more efficient and less reliant on manual labor.

In all these industries, robots help improve safety, reduce costs, and boost productivity. But they don't just do repetitive tasks—they also provide solutions to challenges that humans might face due to fatigue or the need for precision.

Robotic Process Automation (RPA)

Now, let's dive into a slightly different kind of robot: the **Robotic Process Automation** (RPA). RPA isn't a physical robot like the ones we've been talking about, but it's a kind of software that mimics human actions to complete repetitive, rule-based tasks in business operations.

Think of RPA as a **digital robot** that works on your computer. For instance, when a company needs to process thousands of invoices, instead of having a human employee manually entering data into a system, RPA software can do this job quickly and accurately. It can handle tasks like transferring data between systems, sending automatic emails, or even updating records in databases—tasks that would take humans hours but can be done by RPA in a fraction of the time.

RPA is already being used in many sectors. In **finance**, it's helping banks process transactions faster. In **customer service**, it's used to respond to simple customer inquiries or to update customer records. RPA saves companies time and money while reducing errors. Essentially, it's like having a digital assistant doing all the boring, repetitive tasks for you.

Autonomous Robots

Now, let's talk about the next level of robots: **autonomous robots**. These aren't robots that follow a pre-programmed list of tasks. Instead, they make their own decisions based on the environment around them. They can analyze data, assess situations, and decide the best course of action—all on their own.

An example you might be familiar with is **self-driving cars**. These cars don't need a human driver because they are equipped with sensors, cameras, and software that allow them to navigate the roads safely. The car continuously makes decisions about when to stop, go, or turn, all while responding to changes in traffic, weather, and road conditions. This is a perfect example of an **autonomous robot** at work.

In **warehouses**, autonomous robots are also becoming more common. These robots move products around without human input, efficiently finding the fastest route to pick up and deliver items. **Drones** are another type of autonomous robot. They are being used in industries like **delivery** to carry packages to customers' homes or even in **agriculture** to monitor crops from the air, spraying pesticides where needed.

The key difference with autonomous robots is that they don't rely on humans to tell them what to do. They can learn from their surroundings and adjust their actions accordingly. This ability to **make decisions** and **adapt** makes them incredibly useful for tasks that require flexibility and real-time adjustments.

The Future of Robotic Automation

As amazing as robots are today, the future of robotics holds even more exciting possibilities. One of the most fascinating advancements is the rise of **collaborative robots**, or **cobots**. These robots are designed to work **alongside humans** in real-time, making them ideal for environments where human interaction is essential but automation is needed.

For example, in manufacturing, a **cobot** might work with a human to assemble a product. The human might place parts on a conveyor belt, and the robot will pick them up and put them together. The beauty of cobots is that they are designed to work safely with humans, adjusting their movements to avoid harm and enhancing productivity.

Cobots can be used in various industries. In **healthcare**, they can assist doctors in surgeries or help with tasks like carrying medical supplies. In **construction**, cobots could help build structures by handling heavy materials while humans focus on complex tasks like design and supervision.

In the future, robots and humans will likely work together more seamlessly. Rather than replacing people, robots will be tools that enhance human abilities and allow us to focus on tasks that require creativity, problem-solving, or emotional intelligence.

Why Robotics Matter for the Future

Robots and automation are becoming central to how industries operate. They are helping businesses become more **efficient**, **accurate**, and **cost-effective**. Whether it's a factory floor, a delivery service, or a hospital, robots are improving the way we work, and the future is filled with even more opportunities for collaboration between humans and machines.

As robots get smarter, we'll see even more ways they can take on complex tasks, from **manufacturing** to **service** and even **creative industries**. What's most exciting is that robots aren't just about doing things faster—they are changing what's possible and opening up new frontiers for innovation, work, and everyday life.

In this chapter, we explored how robots are not only transforming industries but also paving the way for a future where automation and human collaboration go hand in hand. From basic automation to highly autonomous robots making decisions on their own, the future of robotics is incredibly promising, and it's exciting to think about all the new opportunities they will create in the years to come.

XXXVIII

The Future of Robots, AI Agents, and Chatbots

The Convergence of AI Technologies

Imagine a robot that not only does tasks like cleaning your house or delivering groceries but can also hold a meaningful conversation with you. Or think of a chatbot that you usually interact with on your phone or computer, but now it's integrated into a robot in a store, helping you find products and guiding you through your shopping experience. Welcome to the **convergence** of robots, AI agents, and chatbots.

In the past, these technologies often operated in separate silos. **Chatbots** were primarily used on websites or apps to handle customer service tasks. **AI agents** would be embedded in virtual assistants like Siri or Alexa, helping with reminders, information searches, or smart home management. **Robots** were mostly used in industries for things like manufacturing or logistics.

But today, these technologies are starting to blend together. **Service robots**—those humanoid or industrial-looking machines you see in malls, airports, or hospitals—are now being equipped with conversational abilities, just like chatbots. They can interact with people, answer questions, and even understand context to a degree. It's not just about physical work anymore; these robots are becoming more intelligent and human-like in their interactions.

This convergence is making machines smarter and more versatile. A robot in a hotel might greet guests, assist with luggage, and even answer questions about the city—all while having a conversation as smoothly as a human would. This integration of speech, vision, and physical tasks is what makes robots of the future much more lifelike and useful in a variety of scenarios.

AI and Robots in Everyday Life

In the future, AI agents and robots could become an **integral part of our daily lives**. You might already have a **virtual assistant** on your phone or smart speaker, but imagine if these assistants evolved into fully autonomous, physical robots. These robots could handle all sorts of household tasks, from cleaning to cooking to managing home security. Instead of telling your phone to set an alarm or remind you about a meeting, you could have a robot walk into the room, greet you, and provide personalized updates on your schedule and even take care of chores.

Personalized assistants might be able to understand your preferences over time, like how you take your coffee or when you prefer to exercise, and then offer suggestions to improve your day. These robots wouldn't just be limited to mechanical tasks—they could even help with emotional support, like keeping you company when you're feeling lonely or assisting elderly people who need extra care and attention.

We could also see **robots in stores, schools, and public spaces**. For example, an AI-powered robot in a grocery store might walk you through the aisles, offering personalized shopping recommendations and even making the checkout process smoother. Or a robot in a classroom could serve as an assistant to teachers, helping with administrative tasks or offering tailored learning experiences to students.

What makes all of this possible is the combination of **advanced AI** with robotics. The robots of the future won't just be machines following commands—they'll be **interactive**, **adaptive**, and deeply integrated into our daily routines.

Artificial General Intelligence (AGI) and Human-Robot Collaboration

Here's a question that many people are asking: Can robots and AI agents ever reach the level of **Artificial General Intelligence (AGI)**? **AGI** refers to a machine's ability to perform any intellectual task that a human being can do. It's like a robot with the cognitive abilities of a person, one that can think, learn, and adapt to new situations without being specifically programmed for every task.

If robots and AI agents were to achieve AGI, they could go beyond just following orders or handling specific tasks. They could learn how to work alongside humans in much more complex ways. Imagine a robot not only handling a task like assembling a product but also brainstorming new solutions to problems, coming up with innovative ideas, and helping humans make better decisions.

The potential for **human-robot collaboration** would be extraordinary. Robots with AGI could take on roles that require a combination of thinking, learning, and emotional intelligence. For example, in a healthcare setting, a robot with AGI could work alongside doctors and nurses, offering insights based on the latest research and adapting its suggestions to the patient's specific needs. In the workplace, AGI-powered robots could be team members, assisting with decision-making, creative projects, or strategic planning.

However, we are still a long way from achieving AGI. Today's robots and AI agents are still **narrow AI**, meaning they can handle specific tasks but can't yet generalize their knowledge to completely new situations. Achieving AGI is a monumental challenge, but as AI continues to advance, it's becoming an exciting possibility for the future.

The Limitless Potential of Human-AI Relationships

Looking even further ahead, the relationship between humans and AI could become more profound and personal than we can imagine today. What if robots and AI agents could not only perform tasks but also act as companions? Imagine an AI-powered robot that could understand your emotions and offer empathy when you're feeling down. Or picture a chatbot that's not just responding to queries but offering a **personalized** and **supportive conversation** whenever you need it.

AI agents could evolve to become more than just tools—they could act as **personalized companions**, offering support in various forms: emotional, social, educational, or even therapeutic. For example, elderly individuals who live alone could benefit from robots that not only help with daily tasks but also provide **companionship**. In this future, AI could help reduce loneliness, offering meaningful interactions that make people feel cared for.

Even in education, AI could offer a **highly personalized learning experience**, understanding each student's learning style and adapting the material accordingly. In mental health care, AI could play a role in offering **emotional support** or helping with stress and anxiety management.

This **human-AI relationship** could help people live better lives by providing not just assistance but **genuine connections**. In a way, robots and AI could evolve into companions who not only serve practical purposes but also help enrich human experiences.

Looking Ahead

In this chapter, we've explored the exciting future of robots, AI agents, and chatbots. We've seen how these technologies are converging and changing the way we live and work. From **robots that can converse** with us to **AI agents that could act as companions**, the future promises a world where AI is seamlessly integrated into our lives.

The journey toward **AGI** and **human-AI collaboration** is just beginning, and while it might take time, the potential for what we can achieve with intelligent, interactive machines is virtually limitless. As we continue to develop and refine these technologies, we'll likely see even more ways in which robots and AI agents can enhance our daily lives—making them safer, more enjoyable, and more productive.

The future is incredibly bright, and it's exciting to think about all the new possibilities AI will bring to the table. The next chapter in AI's evolution is just around the corner, and it promises to be a transformative one.

XXXIX

Case Studies and Real-Life Impact of Robots, AI Agents, and Chatbots

In this chapter, we're going to take a closer look at how **robots**, **AI agents**, and **chatbots** are not just futuristic concepts—they're already making a big impact in various industries. By looking at some real-life examples, we'll see how these technologies are changing the way businesses operate, and more importantly, how they're improving lives and making processes more efficient.

Case Study 1: AI in Healthcare

Healthcare is one of the areas where **AI agents** and **robots** are truly making a difference, both for medical professionals and patients alike. Imagine a doctor performing a surgery. While doctors are highly trained, even they can make mistakes, especially in complex procedures. Enter **surgical robots**—robots that assist with precision, control, and minimally invasive surgeries. These robots, like **Intuitive Surgical's da Vinci system**, allow surgeons to make incredibly precise movements, sometimes in very delicate operations, reducing the risk for patients and speeding up recovery times.

But robots aren't just helping in surgery. **AI agents** like **IBM Watson Health** are changing the way doctors diagnose and treat illnesses. IBM Watson has access to vast amounts of medical data and research. It can analyze this information much faster than a human doctor, helping identify patterns, suggest treatment options, and even predict patient outcomes. Watson can even assist in personalized treatment plans based on an individual's medical history and genetic makeup. For example, it's been used to help detect **cancer** more accurately by comparing patient data to vast medical databases.

Robots and AI are also revolutionizing the **administrative side of healthcare**, a place where inefficiencies often occur. AI-powered chatbots are used for **patient scheduling**, answering common questions, and even following up on post-surgery care. These bots reduce the burden on human staff, allowing them to focus on more complex tasks, while patients enjoy quicker responses and a smoother experience.

In essence, healthcare is becoming more efficient, precise, and personalized thanks to AI and robotics. **Patient care is improving**, and **doctors are getting smarter support** to make better decisions.

Case Study 2: AI in Retail and Customer Service

Next, let's talk about how **AI agents** and **chatbots** are transforming the **retail** industry, particularly in the world of **customer service**. If you've ever used **Amazon's Alexa**, you're already familiar with an AI agent that helps with everything from shopping to setting reminders and controlling your smart home devices. Alexa is an example of how AI agents can simplify daily tasks.

But what about when you need help with something specific, like tracking an order or understanding how a product works? Many companies are using **chatbots** to handle customer service inquiries. Chatbots are powered by **Natural Language Processing (NLP)**, which allows them to understand and respond to human language in a natural way. They can answer simple questions, solve issues like forgotten passwords, or even provide personalized shopping recommendations based on your past purchases.

Take **Sephora**, for example. The beauty retailer uses a chatbot to help customers choose the right makeup products based on their preferences, skin type, and even current trends. Chatbots can also be used to assist with

online returns, **processing orders**, or answering FAQs, which means customers don't need to wait for human agents. They can get instant responses 24/7, no matter where they are.

In **e-commerce**, chatbots are helping businesses increase efficiency, while **AI agents** like Alexa are making shopping experiences easier and more enjoyable. For example, you can ask Alexa to order your groceries or schedule a delivery, and the AI will take care of it—just like having your own personal assistant.

This shift towards AI-driven customer service is allowing businesses to offer better **customer experiences** while reducing operational costs. The result? Faster, smarter service that's available around the clock.

Case Study 3: Robots in Manufacturing and Logistics

The **manufacturing** and **logistics** industries are also experiencing a major transformation thanks to robots and AI. Think about the last time you bought something online—how did it get to you so quickly? A lot of the credit goes to robots.

In **warehouses**, robots are increasingly taking on tasks that used to require human labor. Companies like **Amazon** have deployed thousands of robots in their warehouses to help move products from shelves to packaging stations. These robots work alongside humans, picking up heavy or hard-to-reach items and transporting them efficiently across vast storage areas. **Autonomous robots**, like those used by **Amazon Robotics**, can navigate the warehouse on their own, avoiding obstacles, and organizing inventory without needing constant human supervision. This speeds up the entire **supply chain process** and reduces human error.

Then there are **delivery robots** and **drones**, which are starting to make deliveries faster and more efficiently. For example, in some cities, **drones** are now being used to deliver packages, cutting down delivery times and reducing the need for traditional delivery trucks. These robots and drones are also helping companies like **FedEx** and **UPS** optimize their logistics networks.

One of the most exciting developments is the use of **collaborative robots** or **cobots**. These robots work side-by-side with humans, assisting in tasks like assembling products, packaging, and quality control. Unlike traditional robots, which are often kept in separate, restricted areas, cobots can work in more flexible, dynamic environments alongside humans. They're designed to be safe, efficient, and adaptable, making them a valuable addition to the modern factory floor.

In logistics, the combination of AI, robots, and autonomous vehicles is dramatically changing how goods are produced, stored, and delivered, increasing both speed and accuracy while cutting costs and improving safety.

The Big Picture: Real-World Impact

These three case studies—**healthcare**, **retail**, and **manufacturing/ logistics**—demonstrate how robots, AI agents, and chatbots are already improving various industries. While the technologies are still evolving, we're seeing them make tangible differences in **efficiency**, **accuracy**, and **customer satisfaction**.

The **impact** of these innovations isn't limited to businesses—they're benefiting **individuals** too, whether it's through better healthcare, faster and smarter shopping, or quicker delivery of goods.

As we move forward, expect these technologies to become even more integrated into our lives. The possibilities are endless, and as AI continues to develop, we can expect even more **exciting breakthroughs** that will continue to **shape the way we live and work**.

The Societal Impact of AI and Generative AI

XL

Transforming the Workplace with AI

The workplace is not what it used to be, and the pace of change is accelerating. As **artificial intelligence (AI)** continues to advance, it's becoming clear that if you don't adapt, you could quickly find yourself on the outside looking in. **AI is not just a tool anymore**—it's becoming the backbone of how businesses operate, how work is done, and even how companies hire. If you're not leveraging AI in your daily tasks, there's a real risk that your skills could be replaced or deemed irrelevant.

In this chapter, we'll explore how AI is reshaping industries and why using AI in your job is no longer optional. It's essential to keep up if you want to stay relevant in the modern job market.

The Future of Work: AI in Automation and Augmentation

The future of work is here, and it's powered by AI. The two main forces driving this transformation are **automation** and **augmentation**.

Automation means machines or software taking over tasks that were traditionally done by humans. Imagine robots assembling products on an assembly line, or AI systems automatically processing data and making decisions. It's happening in industries across the board—from manufacturing to finance—and it's making businesses more efficient, faster, and cost-effective. If you're still doing tasks that AI can easily handle, you're at risk of being left behind.

But AI doesn't just replace jobs—it **augments** them. This means AI can help you do your job **better**. It acts as a supercharged assistant, boosting your productivity and decision-making abilities. If you're in **finance**, AI can help analyze complex data to predict market trends. If you're in **healthcare**, AI can assist in diagnosing diseases with higher accuracy than ever before. But here's the kicker: **AI will make you more valuable** only if you know how to work with it. If you don't use it, you'll be stuck doing outdated tasks, while others move forward.

How AI is Reshaping Industries: Finance, Manufacturing, and Law

Let's take a closer look at how **AI is changing industries**, and how failing to embrace these technologies could make your job obsolete:

1. Finance

AI is revolutionizing **finance**. Think about it: robo-advisors are now providing personalized investment advice at a fraction of the cost of a human advisor. AI systems can predict stock trends, automate trading, and even spot **fraud**. If you're working in finance and you're not using AI tools, you're falling behind. **Automating simple tasks** like data entry or basic analysis means you have time to focus on more complex, high-value work. If you don't adapt, others will.

2. Manufacturing

Manufacturing is another area where AI is taking over. AI-driven robots are already handling assembly lines and quality checks more efficiently than humans. Drones and self-driving trucks are becoming a common sight in warehouses and logistics, and they're only getting smarter. If you're still working in a role that doesn't embrace AI, your job could be the next to go.

And it's not just about robots replacing human workers. It's about **collaboration**. Robots and AI systems are now working **alongside humans**, making the work safer, faster, and more accurate. If you're not collaborating with AI in your role, you're missing out on an opportunity to become more valuable.

3. Law

AI is reshaping the **legal industry** too. **Document review**, legal research, and even contract analysis can now be done faster and more accurately by AI. Lawyers are using AI to sift through mountains of legal data in seconds, allowing them to focus on strategy and client interaction. If you're in the legal field and you're not using AI tools, you're at risk of becoming outdated and being replaced by those who are.

The Impact of AI on Job Creation, Displacement, and New Roles

Here's the hard truth: **AI will take jobs**. Many repetitive, manual, and rule-based jobs will disappear as robots and AI systems step in. However, that's not the whole story. While AI replaces certain tasks, it's also creating new opportunities and roles. But here's the catch—**those new roles will require new skills**.

For instance, if you're not learning about **AI programming**, **data science**, or **machine learning**, you'll be left behind. The jobs of tomorrow will require **AI literacy**, the ability to work alongside AI, and even the ability to **manage and design AI systems**.

AI is creating jobs in areas like **AI ethics**, **data analysis**, and **system design**. There will be a growing need for people who can ensure AI is used responsibly, design smarter systems, and interpret AI-generated insights. If you're not preparing for these roles, someone else will, and they'll get the job instead of you.

Even jobs that AI can't fully take over will be impacted. In **marketing**, AI tools can optimize ad campaigns or analyze customer behavior, but it's still human creativity that makes the campaigns successful. The key is knowing how to **integrate AI** into your work.

Looking Ahead: The Changing Workplace

AI isn't a far-off futuristic concept. It's here, and it's changing everything. The workplace of tomorrow will be collaborative, where humans and AI work side by side. But this future is only for those who **embrace AI** and learn to adapt. If you're not learning how to use AI to improve your work, you're putting your job at risk. **AI is not just a tool anymore—it's a necessity**.

The bottom line is simple: If you're not using AI to enhance your role, you could find yourself out of the job market. AI is here to stay, and the companies that use it effectively will thrive. Don't get left behind—**start learning how to use AI today** and stay ahead of the curve. The future of work is waiting for those who are ready to adapt.

XLI
Ethical and Social Implications of AI and Generative AI

As **artificial intelligence (AI)** and **generative AI** continue to make their way into almost every part of our lives, they bring along not just excitement, but also a host of **ethical** and **social** concerns. These technologies are powerful, yes, but they also come with challenges that we need to face head-on. In this chapter, we'll explore some of the biggest **ethical dilemmas** that AI presents, and what we must do to ensure that it benefits everyone without causing harm.

AI is not just about cool gadgets or futuristic tech. It's about **decisions** that affect people's lives—who gets a job, who gets a loan, who gets healthcare, and who doesn't. The way we build, use, and control AI can have a huge impact on **society**, and it's important to understand what that means for all of us.

Bias in AI Models and the Challenge of Fairness

One of the biggest ethical challenges we face with AI today is **bias**. Just like humans, AI can have biases, but the problem is that these biases can often be invisible, and they can have real-world consequences. AI systems are **trained** on data, and if that data contains biases—whether they are racial, gender-based, or socio-economic—the AI will learn and repeat those biases.

For example, an AI system that helps in hiring decisions might unintentionally favor male candidates over female candidates if it's trained on data from companies where men were historically hired more often. Similarly, an AI used in law enforcement might be biased toward certain racial groups, leading to unfair treatment or discrimination.

So, **how do we make AI fair?** The first step is to **recognize** that biases exist, and to make sure the data used to train AI is diverse, balanced, and free from prejudice. This is a huge challenge because many times, the data we collect in the real world is already biased. That's why it's important to have **diverse teams** of people working on AI projects to ensure fairness and avoid perpetuating harmful stereotypes.

Ethical Dilemmas in AI Decision-Making

Another major concern with AI is the **decision-making** process. AI is already making decisions in areas like healthcare, criminal justice, and finance. But how do we know if these decisions are fair? **AI doesn't have morals or ethics.** It makes decisions based on patterns in data, not on human values.

Take, for instance, AI used in **healthcare** to diagnose diseases or recommend treatments. While AI can process data and make recommendations faster than a human, what happens when the AI misses a diagnosis or gives an inaccurate recommendation? How do we ensure that AI makes decisions that align with human ethical standards, especially when it comes to life-and-death matters?

And let's not forget about **autonomous vehicles**. Self-driving cars need to make split-second decisions in situations where human lives are at risk. For example, if a self-driving car has to choose between hitting a pedestrian or swerving into a wall, what should it do? **Whose safety should come first?** These are questions that don't have easy answers, and AI can't make those decisions alone. It's up to **society** to decide what's ethically acceptable and to guide AI systems in making responsible choices.

Privacy Concerns, Data Security, and the Digital Divide

As AI becomes more powerful, it's also collecting and processing **more data** than ever before. And that data isn't always just numbers or facts—it can be **personal data** about you, your habits, your health, and your preferences.

This raises important **privacy** concerns.

Let's say you use an AI-powered **smart assistant** like Alexa or Siri. These devices listen to your conversations to improve their performance. But what happens if someone hacks into the system and steals that data? What if your personal information is used in ways you didn't agree to? Protecting **data privacy** is critical, and without strong safeguards, there's a risk that sensitive information could be misused or exploited.

In addition, not everyone has the same access to AI technology. This is what we call the **digital divide**—the gap between those who have access to the internet and advanced technology, and those who don't. As AI continues to grow, there's a real concern that this divide will widen, leaving certain groups of people behind in terms of access to education, healthcare, jobs, and other opportunities. **How do we ensure that AI is accessible to all**, and that no one is left out of the technological revolution?

What Can We Do?

The good news is that we **can** address these concerns. It's up to **governments**, **businesses**, and **individuals** to work together to create policies and regulations that ensure AI is used ethically and responsibly. Some steps include:

1. **Transparency**: AI systems should be transparent. People should be able to understand how AI makes decisions, especially when it affects their lives.
2. **Accountability**: If an AI system makes a mistake, there should be someone responsible for it. Humans need to remain in control and able to intervene if necessary.
3. **Privacy Protections**: Data must be protected, and individuals should have control over their personal information. Consent is key.
4. **Bias Mitigation**: It's crucial to regularly check AI systems for biases and make adjustments to ensure they are fair and inclusive.
5. **Education and Accessibility**: We need to make sure that everyone has the opportunity to learn about AI and access its benefits. This means bridging the digital divide and ensuring that AI doesn't leave anyone behind.

Looking Ahead: A Balanced Approach

The rise of AI and generative AI offers exciting possibilities, but it also brings complex ethical challenges. As we move forward, it's essential to create a balance between **innovation** and **responsibility**. AI should be developed with a strong sense of ethics and a commitment to fairness, privacy, and accessibility. Only then can we ensure that AI works for the benefit of **everyone**, not just a select few.

AI will continue to evolve, and its impact will only grow. But as we shape the future, let's remember that technology should always serve **human** values. By addressing the ethical and social implications head-on, we can ensure that AI enriches our lives without sacrificing the things that matter most—**fairness, privacy, and equity**.

XLII

Regulation and Governance of AI and Generative AI

As AI and **generative AI** become more integrated into our daily lives, the need for proper **regulation** and **governance** becomes more urgent. These technologies hold incredible potential, but without clear rules and guidelines, they can also pose risks. Imagine a world where AI systems, like self-driving cars, healthcare bots, or social media algorithms, are running unchecked. They could make decisions that affect people's lives without any accountability. This is why the **regulation** of AI is so important.

In this chapter, we'll talk about why AI regulation is necessary, what it involves, and how governments, organizations, and international bodies are coming together to shape the future of AI in a safe, fair, and ethical way.

The Need for Global Regulations and AI Ethics

AI is a powerful tool, but with great power comes great responsibility. Just like any technology that impacts society—whether it's the internet, nuclear power, or medical treatments—AI needs **rules** to prevent misuse and ensure it is used ethically. This is where **global regulations** come in.

While AI technologies are being developed all over the world, not all countries have the same laws or regulations. This can create problems, especially when AI systems cross borders, like social media platforms or global data networks. For example, a chatbot trained on data from one country may be used in another country with different cultural values. What happens if this chatbot provides advice or makes decisions that are inappropriate or harmful in that second country? Without **global regulations**, these discrepancies can lead to issues like **bias**, **inequality**, and **misuse of power**.

That's why we need a **global framework** for regulating AI. International bodies, like the **United Nations (UN)** or the **European Union (EU)**, are already taking steps to create common rules for AI. For instance, the EU has proposed guidelines that would classify AI systems by risk—low-risk AI, like AI used in video games, would have fewer regulations, while high-risk AI, like AI used in healthcare or law enforcement, would have stricter rules. The goal is to ensure that AI is **safe**, **fair**, and **transparent** for everyone, no matter where they live.

But regulations aren't just about rules—they're also about ethics. As we talked about earlier, AI systems can sometimes be biased or make decisions that don't align with human values. This is why **AI ethics** is so crucial. AI must be developed with a strong moral foundation, ensuring it supports values like **fairness**, **respect for privacy**, and **inclusivity**. Ethical AI means making sure that AI doesn't cause harm, that it's **transparent** in how it works, and that it doesn't unintentionally favor one group of people over another.

Privacy Laws and AI Accountability

When AI systems are used, they often handle a lot of **personal data**—from medical records to shopping habits, location data, and even conversations. This makes **privacy** one of the biggest concerns with AI. Without proper safeguards, there's a risk that AI could invade people's privacy or misuse their data.

This is where **privacy laws** come into play. In many countries, governments have passed laws to protect people's personal information, like the **General Data Protection Regulation (GDPR)** in the EU. The GDPR ensures that companies must ask for your consent before collecting or processing your personal data, and that they must be transparent about how your data is used.

However, when it comes to AI, **data protection** becomes even more important. AI systems can process vast amounts of personal data, sometimes without the user even realizing it. For instance, smart devices like **voice assistants** or **social media algorithms** may collect your data to improve performance, but how do you know if this data is being stored safely or used ethically?

That's where **accountability** comes in. AI systems need to be **accountable** for how they use data. If something goes wrong—say, if a biased AI makes an unfair decision about someone's job application—who is responsible? Is it the company that created the AI? Is it the developers who programmed it? Or is it the AI itself? These are questions that regulators are trying to answer. Companies need to take responsibility for the actions of their AI systems, and individuals need to have a say in how their data is used.

The Role of Governments and Organizations in Shaping AI Policies

Governments and **regulatory organizations** play a huge role in shaping how AI is developed, used, and governed. Without proper oversight, AI could evolve in ways that harm society, violate privacy, or reinforce inequalities. That's why governments must be proactive in creating policies and frameworks that guide AI's development.

Governments need to establish **clear rules** about how AI can be used. This includes creating laws that **protect privacy**, ensure **accountability**, and prevent discrimination. They also need to **enforce** these laws by setting up independent agencies that monitor AI's impact and compliance.

In addition, governments can collaborate with **international organizations**, like the **World Economic Forum (WEF)**, the **OECD (Organisation for Economic Co-operation and Development)**, and others, to develop **global AI standards**. This collaboration ensures that AI is regulated across borders and that the technology benefits everyone, not just the most powerful nations.

Private organizations also have a part to play. Many large tech companies, such as **Google**, **Microsoft**, and **IBM**, have already created internal AI guidelines and ethical principles for the development and use of their AI systems. These companies are often at the forefront of developing AI, and by adopting responsible practices, they can lead the way for others in the industry.

However, while **corporations** can set their own rules, governments must ensure that the rules are **fair** and **public-facing**. There must be **transparency** about how AI is used and who benefits from it. **Public involvement** is key here—policies and regulations should involve input from a wide range of stakeholders, including **citizens**, **activists**, **ethicists**, and **experts** in fields like **law**, **data protection**, and **human rights**.

Looking Ahead: A Balanced and Responsible Approach

AI has the potential to revolutionize our world, but we must make sure it is developed and used in ways that are safe, ethical, and fair for all. To achieve this, we need strong **regulations** and **governance** that protect people's rights, ensure privacy, and prevent harm.

AI regulation is not just about imposing restrictions—it's about creating a framework that encourages innovation while also protecting the **public interest**. With the right policies, AI can be used to solve some of the world's biggest challenges, from improving healthcare to addressing climate change and solving social inequalities. But this requires cooperation between **governments**, **organizations**, and **individuals** to ensure that AI is developed responsibly.

In the future, as AI continues to evolve, we must all stay vigilant and involved in shaping its direction. By doing so, we can ensure that AI's benefits are shared by everyone, and that it remains a positive force in society.

XLIII

The Potential and Risks of AI and Generative AI

Artificial Intelligence (AI) and **Generative AI** hold immense potential to improve human life in ways we've never seen before. From making healthcare more accessible to transforming how we work and communicate, the possibilities seem endless. But with great power comes great responsibility. While AI offers incredible benefits, it also comes with risks that need to be understood and managed carefully.

In this chapter, we'll explore both the **optimistic view** of AI—the ways it can enhance our lives—and the **risks** that come with it. We'll also discuss how we can **manage** and **mitigate** these risks, ensuring that AI works for the greater good.

The Optimistic View: AI Enhancing Human Life

AI has already begun to make our lives easier, and its potential is only growing. Imagine a world where machines handle the repetitive, time-consuming tasks we don't want to do, leaving us more time to focus on creativity, innovation, and meaningful work. AI systems are already being used in **healthcare**, **education**, **transportation**, and many other industries to make life better.

Healthcare is one of the most promising areas where AI is already having a major impact. AI algorithms can **analyze medical images**, **diagnose diseases**, and even suggest treatment plans, sometimes with greater accuracy than human doctors. For example, AI can scan X-rays to identify early signs of **cancer**, something that might be missed by the human eye. This kind of technology could help doctors detect diseases earlier, saving lives.

In **education**, AI-powered systems are helping students learn at their own pace. For instance, AI can create personalized learning plans based on a student's strengths and weaknesses, making education more accessible and tailored to each individual. In fact, AI tutors can provide students with feedback on their work, helping them improve faster than traditional methods.

In **transportation**, self-driving cars powered by AI are already being tested and, in some cases, are already on the road. These cars promise to reduce accidents caused by human error, improve traffic flow, and make transportation more efficient. Imagine a future where you can relax during your commute while your car takes care of the driving!

Even in **daily life**, AI is enhancing convenience. Smart assistants like **Alexa**, **Siri**, and **Google Assistant** help us manage our schedules, set reminders, and control smart home devices—all with just our voice. AI-powered recommendation systems suggest products we might like, movies we might enjoy, and even help us discover new music.

But what's exciting is that **Generative AI**, a subset of AI, takes things even further. It can **create content**—writing articles, generating artwork, composing music, and even designing products. This technology has the potential to revolutionize creativity by providing new tools for artists, writers, and designers.

The Risks of AI: From Algorithmic Bias to the Misuse of Generative AI

While AI can bring about incredible benefits, it also carries significant risks that we must carefully consider and address.

One of the biggest concerns with AI is **algorithmic bias**. AI systems are trained on data, and if the data they're trained on is biased, the AI will likely produce biased results. For example, if an AI system is trained on data that mostly includes white males, it may not perform as well when making decisions about women or people from other racial backgrounds. This could lead to unfair outcomes in areas like **hiring**, **criminal justice**, and **loan approvals**.

Generative AI also poses a unique set of risks. While it's incredible at creating content, there's the potential for it to be misused. For instance, AI can generate realistic-looking fake images, videos, and even news articles that can be used to deceive or manipulate people. **Deepfakes**, which are fake videos of people saying or doing things they never did, have already been used to spread misinformation and fake news. This raises serious ethical concerns about the misuse of AI for malicious purposes.

Another risk is **privacy**. Many AI systems collect vast amounts of personal data to improve their performance, but this data could be used in ways that violate privacy. For example, some AI-powered apps might track your location, your online activity, or even your personal habits. If this data is not properly protected, it could be stolen or misused.

Furthermore, as AI becomes more powerful, there's a concern that it could be used to **automate** jobs, leading to widespread job displacement. While AI can improve efficiency, it could also replace human workers in certain industries, leading to unemployment for those who aren't able to adapt to the changing job market. In this way, the rise of AI could deepen social inequalities if not managed properly.

Lastly, as AI systems become more autonomous, the **accountability** for their actions becomes blurry. If an AI system makes a harmful decision, who is responsible? Is it the developer who created the system? The company that deployed it? Or the AI itself? This lack of accountability is a major concern, especially when AI is involved in sensitive areas like healthcare or criminal justice.

How to Manage and Mitigate AI's Risks

With all these risks, how can we ensure that AI is used responsibly and safely? While AI's potential is huge, it's important to set up systems and guidelines to minimize the risks.

1. **AI Transparency and Accountability**: One of the first steps in managing AI's risks is making sure that the systems are **transparent**. People should be able to understand how AI makes decisions. If an AI system rejects a job application, for example, it should explain why it made that decision. This **accountability** is key to ensuring that AI systems are used ethically and that any mistakes or biases can be traced back and corrected.

2. **Bias Reduction in AI Models**: Developers and data scientists need to work hard to eliminate bias in AI systems. This can be done by training AI on diverse, representative data and continuously testing the system for fairness. By using **diverse datasets**, AI can be made to treat all groups equally, regardless of race, gender, or other factors.

3. **Ethical Guidelines and Standards**: Governments and organizations must work together to set clear **ethical guidelines** for the development and use of AI. These guidelines should focus on **fairness**, **privacy**, **accountability**, and **transparency**. International bodies like the **United Nations** and **European Union** are already setting standards for responsible AI use, and it's important that these rules are followed globally.

4. **Human Oversight**: Even though AI is becoming more autonomous, it's crucial that humans remain in control. There should always be a level of **human oversight** when it comes to high-stakes decisions, like those in healthcare or law enforcement. Humans should be able to intervene if something goes wrong, and the AI's decisions should be monitored regularly.

5. **Education and Job Training**: As AI continues to reshape industries, it's important to focus on **education** and **job retraining** programs to help people adapt. By offering training in AI-related fields, people can learn new skills and take on new roles that AI cannot easily replace. This will ensure that the benefits of AI are shared across society, and it won't lead to mass unemployment.

6. **Regulation**: Strong **AI regulations** should be implemented at both national and international levels. Governments need to create laws that protect privacy, promote fairness, and ensure the safe use of AI. For example, **data protection laws** like the **GDPR** in Europe help ensure that AI companies can't misuse or mishandle people's personal information.

Looking Ahead: Finding Balance

AI and **Generative AI** are transforming the world in remarkable ways. But with these advancements come risks that cannot be ignored. To ensure that AI is a force for good, we must balance **optimism** with **caution**. By taking proactive steps to manage the risks and create **ethical** frameworks, we can harness AI's power while protecting against its potential dangers.

The future of AI is bright, but it's up to all of us—governments, developers, businesses, and citizens—to make sure that it is developed in a way that benefits everyone. Through **transparency**, **accountability**, and **education**, we can unlock the full potential of AI while safeguarding our privacy, jobs, and the future of humanity.

AI and You: A Shared Future

As we stand at the dawn of a new technological era, *AI Made for You* has guided you through the extraordinary journey of Artificial Intelligence—its transformative power, the creative potential of Generative AI, and the promise of Artificial General Intelligence (AGI). From revolutionizing how we learn and work to redefining healthcare, business, and creativity, AI is not merely changing the world; it is **reshaping the very fabric of our lives**—making it smarter, more efficient, and deeply interconnected.

This book is not just an exploration of technological progress but a heartfelt invitation to embrace what lies ahead. AI is no longer the distant dream of science fiction; it is here, and its impact is profound. Whether you're a student discovering new ways to learn, an entrepreneur harnessing AI to innovate, a teacher finding smarter tools to inspire, or someone marveling at AI's possibilities—you now hold the power to shape the future. The role of AI is not to replace us but to **empower us**: to dream bigger, achieve more, and unlock human creativity on a scale we've never imagined.

But this journey is far from complete. With every new breakthrough comes greater responsibility. Ethical questions will arise. Challenges will demand thoughtful solutions. The decisions we make today will determine the AI-powered world of tomorrow. As readers, as creators, and as citizens of this ever-evolving technological landscape, you have a voice—a role to play in ensuring that AI serves us all. Use this knowledge with care. Innovate boldly. Create meaningfully. And, most importantly, **never lose sight of the human values that must guide this transformation**.

In closing, I ask you to reflect on this: *The future of AI isn't something to be feared or merely observed—it is something to be built, nurtured, and shared.*

Together, let us create a future where AI amplifies our humanity, strengthens our connections, and inspires a brighter, more inclusive world for generations to come.

This is our time to shape what's next. Let's make it extraordinary.

Bibliography And References

Books:

1. **Russell, S., & Norvig, P.** (2020). *Artificial Intelligence: A Modern Approach* (4th ed.). Pearson Education.

   - A leading textbook explaining AI principles, search algorithms, knowledge representation, and machine learning.

2. **Goodfellow, I., Bengio, Y., & Courville, A.** (2016). *Deep Learning*. MIT Press.

   - Fundamental concepts on neural networks, deep learning, and generative models.

3. **Mitchell, M.** (2019). *Artificial Intelligence: A Guide for Thinking Humans*. Farrar, Straus and Giroux.

   - A balanced exploration of AI systems, their progress, limitations, and human impact.

4. **Bostrom, N.** (2014). *Superintelligence: Paths, Dangers, Strategies*. Oxford University Press.

   - A critical analysis of Artificial General Intelligence (AGI) and its future implications.

5. **Ford, M.** (2015). *Rise of the Robots: Technology and the Threat of a Jobless Future*. Basic Books.

   - Discusses AI-driven automation and the resulting workforce disruption.

6. **Kelsey, T.** (2020). *The Creativity Code: How AI is Learning to Write, Paint, and Think*. Pegasus Books.

○ Investigates AI's ability to generate art, music, and creative writing.

7. **Brynjolfsson, E., & McAfee, A.** (2014). *The Second Machine Age: Work, Progress, and Prosperity in a Time of Brilliant Technologies*. W.W. Norton & Company.

   ○ Analyzes how AI and automation transform industries and economies.

8. **Tegmark, M.** (2017). *Life 3.0: Being Human in the Age of Artificial Intelligence*. Knopf.

   ○ Explores AI's societal and ethical challenges as it becomes more advanced.

9. **Miller, J. H., & Page, S. E.** (2007). *Complex Adaptive Systems: An Introduction to Computational Models of Social Life*. Princeton University Press.

   ○ Explains AI systems' adaptability in dynamic environments.

10. **Christian, B.** (2020). *The Alignment Problem: Machine Learning and Human Values*. W.W. Norton & Company.

    ○ Discusses the alignment of machine learning models with human ethics and values.

11. **Harari, Y. N.** (2018). *21 Lessons for the 21st Century*. Spiegel & Grau.

    ○ Includes reflections on AI's role in the future of work, privacy, and decision-making.

12. **Floridi, L.** (2014). *The Ethics of Information*. Oxford University Press.

    ○ A philosophical perspective on AI ethics, privacy, and misinformation.

13. **Domingos, P.** (2015). *The Master Algorithm: How the Quest for the Ultimate Learning Machine Will Remake Our World*. Basic Books.

- Explores the potential of machine learning to revolutionize industries.

14. **Nilsson, N. J.** (2009). *The Quest for Artificial Intelligence: A History of Ideas and Achievements.* Cambridge University Press.

   - A historical overview of AI development.

Academic Papers and Research Articles:

1. **LeCun, Y., Bengio, Y., & Hinton, G.** (2015). "Deep Learning." *Nature,* 521(7553), 436–444.

   - Seminal work introducing deep learning principles and their applications.

2. **Goodfellow, I., Pouget-Abadie, J., Mirza, M., et al.** (2014). "Generative Adversarial Networks." *NeurIPS.*

   - The foundational paper on Generative Adversarial Networks (GANs).

3. **Radford, A., Wu, J., Child, R., et al.** (2019). "Language Models are Unsupervised Multitask Learners." *OpenAI GPT-2 Technical Report.*

   - GPT-2 and its ability to perform unsupervised tasks with human-like fluency.

4. **Brown, T., Mann, B., Ryder, N., et al.** (2020). "Language Models are Few-Shot Learners." *NeurIPS 2020.*

   - Introduction of GPT-3, demonstrating significant advances in large language models.

5. **Schmidhuber, J.** (2015). "Deep Learning in Neural Networks: An Overview." *Neural Networks,* 61, 85-117.

   - Comprehensive overview of neural networks and deep learning history.

6. **Van den Oord, A., Kalchbrenner, N., & Kavukcuoglu, K.** (2016). "Pixel Recurrent Neural Networks." *ICML.*

   ◦ Introduced generative models for image generation.

7. **Reed, S., Akata, Z., Yan, X., et al.** (2016). "Generative Adversarial Text to Image Synthesis." *ICML 2016.*

   ◦ Early development of text-to-image generation models.

8. **Zellers, R., Holtzman, A., Bisk, Y., et al.** (2019). "Defending Against Neural Fake News." *NeurIPS.*

   ◦ Discusses challenges with misinformation generated by AI.

9. **Ethayarajh, K.** (2019). "How Contextual are Contextualized Word Representations?" *EMNLP 2019.*

   ◦ Insights into how transformers understand and generate text.

Web Resources and Reports:

1. **OpenAI.** (2022). "Introducing ChatGPT." Retrieved from: https://openai.com/blog/chatgpt

   ◦ Official introduction and description of ChatGPT.

2. **McKinsey Global Institute.** (2023). "The State of AI in 2023: Progress, Promise, and Challenges." Retrieved from: https://www.mckinsey.com

   ◦ Comprehensive insights into AI trends, challenges, and economic impact.

3. **Ng, A.** (2017). *AI is the New Electricity.* TED Talk. Retrieved from: https://www.ted.com.

   ◦ Highlights AI's transformative power across industries.

4. **Google Research.** (2023). "AI in Healthcare: Detecting Diabetic Retinopathy." Retrieved from: https://ai.googleblog.com.

    ◦ AI applications in healthcare.

5. **MIT Technology Review.** (2023). "Generative AI: What It Is, Tools, and Applications." Retrieved from: https://www.technologyreview.com.
6. **IBM Research.** (2023). "AI Ethics and Trust." Retrieved from: https://www.ibm.com/ai/ethics.
7. **World Economic Forum.** (2023). "AI and the Future of Work." Retrieved from: https://www.weforum.org.
8. **Stanford University.** (2023). *AI Index Report 2023*. Retrieved from: https://aiindex.stanford.edu.

    ◦ Annual report on AI research, development, and adoption.

www.ingramcontent.com/pod-product-compliance
Lightning Source LLC
Chambersburg PA
CBHW051153130726
47988CB00005B/2103